USDA

United States
Department of
Agriculture

Forest Service

Pacific Southwest
Research Station

General Technical
Report
PSW-GTR-231

October 2010

Twenty-Five Years of Managing Vegetation in Conifer Plantations in Northern and Central California: Results, Application, Principles, and Challenges

Philip M. McDonald and Gary O. Fiddler

Pesticide Precautionary Statement

This publication reports research involving pesticides. It does not contain recommendations for their use, nor does it imply that the uses discussed here have been registered. All uses of pesticides must be registered by appropriate state or federal agencies, or both, before they can be recommended.

CAUTION: Pesticides can be injurious to humans, domestic animals, desirable plants, and fish or other wildlife—if they are not handled or applied properly. Use all pesticides selectively and carefully. Follow recommended practices for the disposal of surplus pesticides and pesticide containers.

Authors

Philip M. McDonald is a research forester (emeritus), Pacific Southwest Research Station, Western Forest Management Unit, 3644 Avtech Parkway, Redding, CA 96002; e-mail: pmcdonald@fs.fed.us; and **Gary O. Fiddler** is a silviculturist, Ecosystem Conservation Staff; Pacific Southwest Region, Vallejo, and stationed at the above address in Redding, CA; e-mail: gfiddler@fs.fed.us.

Cover photographs are by the authors.

Abstract

McDonald, Philip M.; Fiddler, Gary O. 2010. Twenty-five years of managing vegetation in conifer plantations in northern and central California: results, application, principles, and challenges. Gen. Tech. Rep. PSW-GTR-231. Albany, CA: U.S. Department of Agriculture, Forest Service, Pacific Southwest Research Station. 87 p.

In the late 1970s, the outlook for conifer seedlings in new plantations in the Western United States was dismal—too many were dying or growing below the potential of the site. This situation was untenable, and a large study aimed at increasing the survival and growth of planted conifer seedlings was implemented. This was the National Administrative Study on Vegetation Management of which the California portion is reported here. This "study" was really a program on plantation release with 32 individual studies that resulted in more than 60 publications over a 25-year timeframe. The authors emphasized plant community development and biological influences to help explain why some direct release methods were effective and some were not. Survival and growth of several species of conifer seedlings were correlated to the density, foliar cover, and height of various combinations of over 235 species of hardwoods, shrubs, forbs, and graminoids after application of five principal release techniques (herbicides, manual release, mulches, grazing, and mechanical [large machines]). Herbicide use was the most effective treatment followed by manual release and mulches. Domestic grazing, as currently practiced, was not effective, and release with large machines was worthwhile only if followed by an herbicide. Genetic enhancement of conifer seedlings showed promise as a vegetation management tool at first, but lost its efficacy later. Indirect vegetation management by using shade and organic material to reduce the growth and density of competing vegetation has potential, but needs more study. Nineteen principles and 10 conclusions resulted from this research program, but more work in the form of 11 challenges is recommended.

Keywords: Competing vegetation, conifer seedling growth, northern California, plant community dynamics, vegetation management.

Summary

Inadequate reforestation and poor conifer seedling survival and growth led to a national research and application program on vegetation management in young conifer plantations. Findings from the California part of this program, and more specifically on plantation release, are presented here. Results are from 32 study sites throughout northern and central California and reported in more than 60 publications over a 25-year timeframe. The study sites represent a wide variety of site qualities, soils, slopes, aspects, and vegetation types. Most of the planted conifer seedlings were ponderosa pine (*Pinus ponderosa* Dougl. ex Laws. var. *ponderosa*) and Douglas-fir (*Pseudotsuga menziesii* [Mirb.] Franco var. *menziesii*).

We wanted to bring a more holistic perspective to vegetation management, and to concentrate on plant community development, biological influences, and operational techniques. The goal was to describe what plant species are present in young conifer plantations, how they and the communities they represent develop, and how they can be manipulated to achieve vegetation management goals. Consequently, in addition to vegetation management, we present information on botany, ecology, wildlife, domestic grazing, and economics (costs).

Knowing which are the most competitive species in the plant community mandates knowledge on what species are present in young conifer plantations—a subject heretofore not well known. In one study on a good site, a total of 71 plant species were found during the 5-year study, although no more than 62 were present during a given year. Every plant species was measured for density, foliar cover, and average dominant height every year. After 5 years, density averaged 112,408 plants per acre, foliar cover 17,433 ft^2 per acre, and height from 0.8 ft for perennials to 2.4 ft for graminoids. In another more extensive study with 21 study areas (plantations) each with 10 years of data, the average number of plant species in each plantation was 23 at the beginning and 28 at the end. For all the plantations combined, more than 235 species in six categories (conifers, hardwoods, shrubs, forbs, graminoids, and ferns) were found at the beginning and 213 at the end of the study. Core species and genera (defined as being present in at least 50 percent of plantations) numbered 3 and 10, respectively.

The morphological and physiological adaptations of some species enable them to capture scarce resources such as soil moisture, nutrients, and growing space almost from the beginning of their existence. They also can tolerate extreme stress. For example, 5-year-old deerbrush (*Ceanothus integerrimus* Hook. & Arn.) seedlings can withstand an internal moisture stress of 42.7 atmospheres and greenleaf manzanita seedlings (*Arctostaphylos patula* E. Greene) one of 23.8 atmospheres without apparent damage. In a 4-year side-by-side study of these two species, deerbrush developed a clump of stems the first growing season and greenleaf manzanita the second. By the end of the second season, deerbrush had produced statistically more stems per plant, was taller, and had wider crowns than manzanita. Deerbrush also began to produce flowers and seed during the third growing season, but manzanita did not do so during the study. These data suggest that deerbrush is the more competitive species, at least for the first 4 years. In another study, biomass accumulation of 1-year-old greenleaf manzanita plants on a good site was almost 60 times that of ponderosa pine seedlings.

We have found that plants in the early seral community of young conifer plantations in California follow most, if not all, of the five classical regeneration strategies: windblown seeds, persistent seed banks, persistent seedling banks, rapid expansion aboveground, and vegetative elongation belowground. They also embrace one or more of the three traditional successional pathways of facilitation, tolerance, and inhibition. Together the regeneration strategies and successional pathways mean that a large variety of well-adapted plant species, each with unique ability, will be present in young conifer plantations.

This paper details results from nearly all the direct vegetation management release techniques used in the Western United States. These include herbicides, manual release, mulches, grazing (browsing) animals, and mechanical (large machines). Also included are genetic enhancement of young ponderosa pine seedlings and a new concept termed "indirect treatments." We evaluated 21 variations of the direct treatments and 96 trials in this part of our research program.

We found that herbicides are effective for release on a wide range of plant communities at a reasonable cost. Manual release generally is effective if the community is mostly forbs and graminoids, or shrubs if very young. The cost of manual release is higher than for herbicides because a second treatment is often necessary. Mulches are effective if they are large and durable, but are severely limited by cost. As presently practiced, the use of domestic grazing animals for plantation release showed no significant gain in conifer seedling growth. Grazing is too little, too late, and not enough competing vegetation is utilized. Mechanical release of older seedlings with large machines is not effective without a followup application of herbicides.

Genetic enhancement to boost the growth of conifer seedlings over that of competing species began with promise, but deteriorated to the point that it showed little efficacy as a vegetation management tool. Indirect vegetation management using shade and organic material to reduce the growth and density of competing vegetation has promise, but needs more study. It has the advantage of being low in cost and the disadvantage of taking more time to achieve results. No side-by-side studies comparing direct and indirect treatments are known.

Nineteen principles, 11 challenges, and 10 conclusions have come from this study. Some of the most important principles concern developmental variables for conifer seedlings and competing vegetation. In general, seedling height is a poor descriptor of growth, stem diameter is best, and foliar cover of shrubs best explains the most variation in pine seedling parameters. Important challenges concern the need to better predict what competing species will be present in young conifer plantations, and their potential density and size. More knowledge on the below-ground ecosystem is critical. One of the most important conclusions is that conifer plantations in clearcuttings, and herbicides, burning, and grazing are feasible at some place, at some time, and for some purpose. They should remain in the vegetation manager's repertory of available methods and techniques.

Contents

Introduction

In the beginning there was brush, lots of brush, and the plantation manager said: "We won't worry about it for now. If it gets bad, we will treat it later."[1] In the end, the plantation was almost all brush (fig. 1) and the manager said: "If only I had acted earlier"

This heartfelt comment portrays the state of vegetation management in California in its early years. Indecision, frustration, and especially lack of knowledge were commonplace among forest land managers who were trying to establish young conifer plantations that would be fully stocked and growing at the potential of the site. Unfortunately, this goal often was not attained and a trend of disturbingly poor conifer seedling survival and growth was all too apparent. In many plantations, and for several species, conifer seedling survival often was less than 50 percent after three growing seasons. This situation was untenable.

The combination of poor seedling growth in plantations and a court ruling limiting the use of herbicides on national forest (U.S. Department of Agriculture Forest Service) land prompted the Chief and Staff of the Forest Service in Washington, DC, to propose a National Administrative Study in summer 1979 to manipulate competing vegetation in young conifer plantations. The study stressed scientific verification of results from many operational vegetation control techniques. In 1980, the California part of the national administrative study was implemented by the team of researcher Philip McDonald and silviculturist Gary Fiddler, working as a joint endeavor by the Pacific Southwest Research Station and the Pacific Southwest Region of the Forest Service. Initial funding was provided by the National Forest System in Washington, DC, with subsequent financial support by the Pacific Southwest Region. Later, most of the funding was provided by the Pacific Southwest Research Station.

The team was given the broadest possible latitude to develop their study program in terms of number and kind of treatments, experimental design, data manipulation, and presentation of study results. McDonald and Fiddler emphasized plantation release and initially concentrated on chemical (herbicides) and manual manipulation of unwanted vegetation. In 1982, they broadened their research program to include vegetative manipulation by grazing animals and large machines. Still later, mulch mats to inhibit vegetative competition, indirect manipulation of competing vegetation, and genetic enhancement of ponderosa pine (*Pinus ponderosa* Dougl. ex Laws. var. *ponderosa*) seedlings in an attempt to outgrow

> **The combination of poor seedling growth in plantations and a court ruling limiting the use of herbicides on national forest land prompted the Chief and Staff of the Forest Service in Washington, DC, to propose a National Administrative Study in summer 1979 to manipulate competing vegetation in young conifer plantations.**

---

[1] Anonymous. 1983. Comment from audience at 5th annual forest vegetation management conference. Sacramento, CA: November 2–3, 1983.

Figure 1— (A) Choked with brush, seedlings in this ponderosa pine plantation have little chance of growing at the potential of the site. (B) Too much competition and lack of resources have doomed this young pine seedling.

competing vegetation, were added. Implicit in this program was the desire to study "alternatives" for manipulating undesired vegetation in plantations, not only for increasing conifer seedling growth but also for understanding the basic ecology of competing vegetation, crop/weed competition, animal damage, and "to explore likely future issues." Because cost is a major concern to practitioners of vegetation management, data on time to apply the various treatments and concomitant dollar values almost always were recorded. This gave the research study program an economic component as well. Based on all of these components, it was recognized as "The most extensive program in North America to compare all silvicultural alternatives for vegetation management" (Campbell 1991).

Throughout, the study approach was one of constant fine-tuning, based on countless hours of thought and discussion. We strived to incorporate ideas from other natural science disciplines, and from scientists at universities, the Weed Science Society, and vegetation management cooperatives. Results from local and international vegetation management conferences, as well as from related research endeavors such as the Forestry Intensified Research program in southwest Oregon (Tappeiner and others 1992) and the Garden of Eden study in northern California (Powers and Ferrell 1996) were consistently monitored. We were especially interested in bringing a more holistic perspective to managing vegetation in young conifer plantations. Consequently, in addition to vegetation management, we had research components in botany, ecology, fuels, wildlife, and domestic grazing in our study. We also became increasingly aware, particularly in the later years of the study, of the increasing concern about climate change and carbon sequestration. Although we could not change the design of the basic program or the experimental design of the individual studies, we did incorporate these concerns into our manuscripts.

The objectives of this paper are to summarize the methodology, results, and knowledge gleaned from more than 30 studies on the release of young conifer seedlings from undesirable vegetation. Specific objectives were to:

- Present several fundamental processes that influence the development of vegetation.
- Determine plant community development and species richness in young conifer plantations.
- Evaluate manual, chemical, grazing animal, mulch, mechanical, and indirect release treatments and genetic enhancement of young conifer seedlings.
- Understand conifer seedling growth versus weed quantity relationships.

- Arrive at "best" treatments in terms of conifer survival, growth, and cost.
- Present some principles of vegetation management derived from this research program and some challenges facing forest vegetation managers in the near future.

Because of the extensiveness of our study, most of the material in this paper will be from it, but numerous other references are used to augment a finding, make a point, or broaden the discussion. Results from two related longer-term studies (28 and 31 years) in particular are used to help explain important biological relationships. Consequently, this paper is not a summary of all that has been tried by others or is known on manipulating vegetation in young conifer plantations. It is our experience.

Although wide in scope, the program had one major and two minor limitations. The major limitation was that we concentrated on plantation release and not on site preparation. An early, but extensive, survey found that site preparation in the California region was effective and generally well done, but many questions were being asked about plantation release. The first of the minor limitations was that the study was installed in young conifer plantations 1 to 4 years old, except for the mechanical treatment, which involved large machines (Trac Mac, Hydro-Ax[2]) in plantations older than 12 years. The second minor limitation was time. The duration of studies was 10 years if possible, which was about the time that the conifer seedlings would begin to compete with themselves.

A strength and a limitation of the program is its extensive nature. More than 60 publications have been produced. The limitation is that data from some of these publications are not included, nor referenced, in this paper. However, every publication contributed to the results, implications, and discussion presented here.

Location, Site Characteristics, and Treatments

When this research and application program began, research on the ecology and manipulation of many, if not most, of the plant species in young conifer plantations was scant and the information that was available was badly fragmented, anecdotal, or from small unreplicated studies. The strength of this paper is that it is based on plant presence and response data from 32 different study sites located throughout northern and central California (fig. 2). Forty-two studies were planned and located on the ground, but 10 of them were lost for a variety of reasons, including forest fires, chronic deer browsing, and lack of cattle fencing. The 32 studies were

When this research and application program began, research on the ecology and manipulation of many, if not most, of the plant species in young conifer plantations was scant and the information that was available was badly fragmented, anecdotal, or from small unreplicated studies.

---

[2] The use of trade or firm names in the publication is for reader information and does not imply endorsement by the U.S. Department of Agriculture of any product or service.

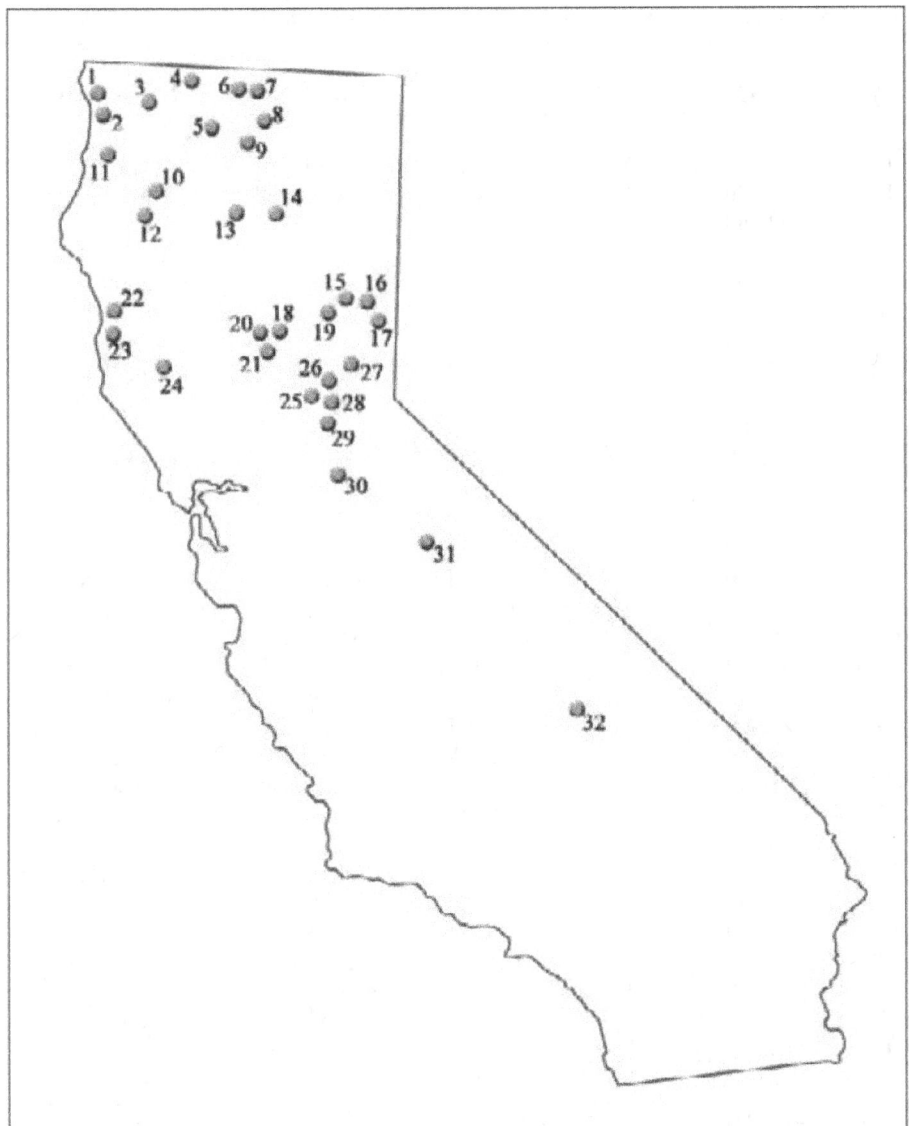

Figure 2—Location of 32 study areas in northern and central California.

located mostly on land administered by the USDA Forest Service, but also on land managed by the USDI Bureau of Land Management, the state of California, Hoopa Indian Reservation, and private industry (Sierra Pacific Industries). Twenty-one of these studies had at least 10 years of data, and several had 5 years of record. All studies had from three to six replications, intensive statistical analysis, and all have been published. Map reference number, study names, species of conifer seedling, elevation, site quality, treatment, and soils (series and texture) describe each study location (table 1). Throughout the paper, the study name is used to reference specific areas.

Table 1—Map (fig. 2), reference number, and information for study areas in northern and central California

Map reference	Study area	Species[a]	Elevation	Site quality[b]	Treatments[c]	Soil series	Soil texture
Number			Feet				
1	Signal	DF	1,500	M	C, H, M	Aiken	Loam, clay loam
2	Rocky	DF	2,550	M	C, H, M	Hugo-Clallam	Gravelly loam
3	Henry Bell	DF	2,400	M	C, H, M	Holland	Shale
4	Hamburg	PP	3,100	L	C, H, M	—	Gravelly loam
5	Trapper	PP	6,200	M	C, M	Scheld-Iller	Sandy loam
6	Stephens Pass A	WF	5,600	M	C, M	Avis	—
7	Stephens Pass B	RF	5,600	M	C, M	Avis	—
8	McBride	PP	4,750	L	C, M	Neer	Sandy loam
9	ElkSprings	PP	4,800	H	C, H, M	Shasta	Loamy sand
10	Harrison Gulch	PP	3,800	L	C, M, Mu	Marpa	Gravelly loam
11	Hoopa	TO	2,690	H	I	—	Loam
12	Mad River	DF	3,250	H	C, M	Holland	Sandy loam
13	Logan	PP	5,000	M	C, H, M	Crazier	Loam
14	Latour	PP	5,200	M	C, H	Windy	—
15	Deans	JP	4,500	H	C, M	Skalan	Sandy loam
16	Lee's Summit	PP, DF	5,000	M	C, H, M	Skalan	Sandy loam
17	Sheep II	JP	6,600	L	C, G, H, M	Haypress	Sandy loam
18	Third Water	PP, JP	5,500	M	C, H, Me	Gibsonville	Sandy loam
19	Mulches	DF	3,600	M	C, Mu	Holland	Sandy loam
20	Alumagel	DF	3,600	M	C, M	Holland	Sandy loam
21	Votaw	PP	4,000	M	C, H, Mu	Cohasset	Loam, clay loam
22	Bear Trap	DF	1,400	H	C, M, Mu	Honeydew	Gravelly loam
23	Nooning Creek	DF	2,300	H	C, M	Honeydew	Gravelly loam
24	Boggs	PP	3,550	M	I	Aiken	Loam, clay loam
25	Snag	PP, DF	3,600	H	C, H, M	Aiken	L oam, clay loam
26	Cattle II	PP	4,250	H	C, G, H	Crozier	Loam, clay loam
27	Sheep I	PP, DF	4,900	M	C, G	Dubakella	—
28	Big Tunnel	PP	4,600	M	C, H, Me	McCarthy	Sandy loam
29	Bear Clover	PP	4,000	H	C, H	Cohasset	Loam
30	Chaix	PP	3,400	M	Ge	Mariposa-Jocal	Loam, clay loam
31 G	rapevine	PP	3,850	M	C, H	Josephine	—
32	Big Collars	PP	5,900	M	C, H, Mu	—	Sandy loam

[a] DF = Douglas-fir, PP = ponderosa pine, WF = California white fir, RF = California red fir, TO = tanoak, JP = Jeffrey pine.
[b] M = medium, L = low, H = high.
[c] C = control, H = herbicide, M = manual, MU = mulch, ME = mechanical, G = grazing, GE = genetics.
— = No data.

All but one of the studies were located in conifer plantations, with seedlings that were planted by hand as bare root or container-grown stock, as opposed to naturally-seeded seedlings. Natural regeneration may occur when seed sources are present at the time of disturbance, but it may not provide the desired species composition, distribution, or density in a timely manner. Planted seedlings almost always accomplish these goals. Ponderosa pine and coast Douglas-fir (*Pseudotsuga menziesii* [Mirb.] Franco var. *menziesii*) were most commonly planted, with Jeffrey pine (*Pinus jeffreyi* Grev. & Balf.), California white fir (*Abies concolor* var. *lowiana*

[Gord.] Lemm.), and California red fir (*A. magnifica* A. Murr.) present in a few studies. Scientific and common names of trees are from Little (1979), and all other vegetation follows the nomenclature of Hickman (1993).

Studies were located throughout northern and central California, specifically from N 41°52'56", W 123°3'26" to N 36°11'23", W 118°39'56". Study locations spanned about 500 mi north to south and about 135 mi east to west. The studies were located in the California Coast Mountains (including the King Range), Klamath Mountains, southern Cascade Range, Diamond Mountains, and Sierra Nevada. Site quality ranged from very high to very low, with most study sites having average quality. An average site would support ponderosa pines that were about 70 ft tall at 50 years of age (Powers and Oliver 1978). The "lowness" of the poorest site was ameliorated somewhat by being on a north slope and receiving an average rainfall of 40 in annually.

Soils were derived from a broad range of parent materials, including volcanic, meta-sedimentary, and igneous rocks. Some soils were deep, fertile, and of high water holding capacity, whereas others were shallow, rocky, and prone to rapid moisture loss. Most were in-between. Textures ranged from loam, clayloam to sandy and gravelly. Taxonomically, soils ranged from Ultic Haploxeralfs to Typic Dystroxerepts.

The climate of the study areas is mediterranean with long, hot, dry summers and cool, moist winters. In most of the plantations, May through October often are dry with little or no effective precipitation. Consequently, the vegetation has adapted over millennia to both a long period of drought and frequent wildfires. Even near the Pacific Ocean, the summers are hot and dry, albeit of shorter duration. Soil moisture is the limiting environmental factor and drought the primary cause of mortality for most plants. Daily summer temperatures varied from 60 to 106 °F. and winter temperatures from -25 to 50 °F. Elevations ranged from 1,400 to 6,600 ft with most occurring in the 4,000- to 5,000-ft range. Average annual precipitation varied from 25 in at a study on the slopes of Mount Shasta to 125 in at a study near the Pacific Ocean. Most studies received precipitation as both rain and snow.

Many species of birds and animals inhabited or roamed through the study areas, but rarely were they seen. Deer (*Odocoileus* spp.) and pocket gophers (*Thomomys* spp.) were the most common species, and in a few instances caused damage. Indeed, one study had to be abandoned because of chronic deer browsing; in another, damage by pocket gophers was serious. Crouch (1979) stated that pocket gophers are "a major cause of reforestation failures in many western conifer forests."

The plantation release treatments included the five classical direct methods of (1) herbicides, (2) manual release, (3) mulches, (4) mechanical (large machines), and (5) grazing animals, as well as genetic enhancement and two indirect techniques (shade and organic material).

The first study plantation was measured in fall 1980, and final data were collected in the last study in 1998. The studies were located in the general forest zone with rocky areas, riparian zones, burned slash piles, and areas near roadsides excluded. All areas had received some form of site preparation or had recently burned in a wildfire. Almost all hardwood trees, clumps of shrubs, logging slash, and unmerchantable conifers were removed during site preparation. Thus, the plantations were characterized initially by full sunlight and only minor amounts of vegetation aboveground. No study sites were treated with soil-active herbicides during site preparation.

As noted earlier, the plantation release treatments included the five classical direct methods of (1) herbicides, (2) manual release, (3) mulches, (4) mechanical (large machines), and (5) grazing animals, as well as genetic enhancement and two indirect techniques (shade and organic material). Each individual study had three to six treatments, usually four. Many treatment variations existed, especially in the herbicide and manual applications. For example, herbicides could consist of any of five different products, and range from application to the whole plot or to either of two different radii. Every study had an untreated control, which of course, had no plantation release cost, and most studies had a near free-to-grow treatment[3] that was the most expensive to install. Other treatments were intermediate and varied in biological effectiveness and cost.

Herbicides—
Commonly applied herbicides were soil-active Velpar, foliage-active Garlon 4, 2,4-D, Roundup, and cutting plus cut-surface-active Garlon 3A. One or two trials were with Arsenal, Escort, and Pronone (granular Velpar). A licensed applicator applied the herbicides, usually in the morning, which most often was the time when specific conditions of wind and temperature were met. Spraying was performed during the summer at a time when growth of the conifer seedlings had ceased, but that of the shrubs, forbs, and grasses was continuing. A guide often was used to ensure uniform coverage of the herbicide and to avoid overlapping and skipped areas.

Manual release—
This direct form of plantation release usually was accomplished with grubbing tools, and, in a few instances, with shears or a chainsaw. Manual release differed even more than herbicides as radii from 1 to 6 ft were grubbed as well as the whole plot. In addition, some plots were treated from 1 to 10 times. Sometimes a manual slashing would take place followed by an herbicide application.

---

[3] In this paper, "free to grow" means almost no competition.

Mulching—

In this research and application program, mulching was aimed primarily at conifer seedling growth; survival was secondary. Seedling survival had been the goal in most prior studies (McDonald and Helgerson 1990), but we wanted to broaden the application of this method. All mulches in our studies were manufactured mats of specific materials and sizes as opposed to applications of wood chips, sand, or sawdust that were areawide. Mulches differed greatly, and early trials (Votaw) were with kraft paper, black and clear plastic, reinforced paper/asphalt sandwiches, pressed peatmoss, and woven and nonwoven polypropylene. Later tests were with various sizes and thicknesses of polyester felt and woven polypropylene. Sizes varied from 1 to 10 ft square.

Mechanical release—

Mechanical release was accomplished with large machines that resembled lawn mowers but with free-swinging rotary cutting heads. These machines were power-ful, stable, and maneuverable. They easily severed the stems of large, tall shrubs and small hardwood trees, and adroitly dodged rocks and stumps in the planted area. Cutting widths were 4 to 8 ft. The Hydro-Ax is an example. It cuts vegetation close to the ground and leaves the chopped stems and other organic material on site. It is efficient on slopes of up to 40 percent, and with a skilled operator is capable of treating 3 to 4 acres per day.

Grazing animals—

Cattle and sheep were the grazing animals in this study. In general, the cattle grazed mostly on grass and the sheep browsed mostly on shrubs, but both kinds of animals did both. Hence for simplicity, we use the more inclusive term "grazing" to describe this direct-release category. The use of cattle to manipulate competing vegetation was planned in three studies. Unfortunately, two of these studies were abandoned because of problems with permittees and fencing. The one study that we had was titled "Cattle II" and was located on the Forest Hill Ranger District of the U.S. Forest Service's Tahoe National Forest. Measurements took place from 1988 through 1997. The herd consisted of 20 to 100 mature cows with calves that roamed through the study area from June through September. Grazing took place in 5 years of the 10-year study. The animals were familiar with mountain topography and wildland grazing.

We had two studies with sheep (Sheep I and II). The bands consisted of 600 to 1,500 animals, mostly nonlactating ewes. In one study, the sheep were experienced with wildland conditions and the plant species in the area; in the other study, they were trucked to an area near the study site, unloaded, and allowed to browse for a week to become accustomed to the wildland environment. A herder and dogs guided the sheep in and out of the allotments (which included the study areas) during the grazing season, which was from June through September. The animals bedded down each night near the study areas where there was water. The animals passed through the study areas about 10 times each year, and, in each pass, grazed no longer than a week.

If genetically improved seedlings outgrow competing shrubs and grasses, especially during the first 3 years after planting, the plantations may not need to be released, or released a second time.

Genetic enhancement—

Genetically improved conifer seedlings, the product of years of selection, progeny testing, and breeding, have potential value for lessening the negative impact of undesirable vegetation in young conifer plantations. If genetically improved seedlings outgrow competing shrubs and grasses, especially during the first 3 years after planting, the plantations may not need to be released, or released a second time. Eliminating release treatments could save millions of dollars in California and perhaps elsewhere, given full implementation of genetically improved planting stock.

Although more were planned, we ended with only one study on genetic enhancement (Chaix). It was with ponderosa pine seedlings. Three classes of enhancement, each with and without competition, were tested for survival and stem growth: (1) nursery run, (2) wind-pollinated, and (3) control-pollinated. Each class was considered a treatment. Nursery-run seedlings were typical seedlings planted in conventional plantations throughout California; wind-pollinated seedlings were from genetically superior females selected from progeny tests with seed collections from natural stands; and control-pollinated seedlings had both males and females selected, based on progeny tests, with the seed collected from a breeding orchard. Control-pollinated seedlings were the best planting stock that would be available for large-scale operations in California for the next two decades. Nursery-run seedlings were from seed collected from several stands in the seed zone corresponding to the elevation of the study. Wind-pollinated seedlings were from four wind-pollinated families. Control-pollinated seedlings were from four full-sib families. All families were in the appropriate or adjacent seed zone.

Seed from each genetic class was sown in spring 1989 in a seedbed at the Forest Service nursery at Placerville, California, with alternating rows of each class perpendicular to the long axis of the bed. To avoid possible bias, sowing rate and seedbed density were similar for each genetic class. All seedlings were transplanted from the nursery to the study site after one season in the nursery and planted by the same workers the same day (March 20, 1990). Each worker planted a different class of seedling in each block (replication) to avoid planting bias. Seedling spacing was 12 by 12 ft in rows with planting spots prepared by augers. Rows were perpendicular to the slope.

Indirect methods—

The indirect strategy of vegetation management is based on modifying the environment to the disadvantage of the weeds. The key to its application is use of natural elements such as organic matter, shade, overstory, and adjacent vegetation to decrease or weaken normally robust and aggressive competing plant species. In an indirect strategy, the environment becomes the treatment.

The use of organic matter to retard germination of dormant seeds in the soil has been reported many times by forest observers and documented in one of our studies on the Plumas National Forest (Lee's Summit). Likewise, the effect of shade has been observed to dramatically slow the growth of aggressive shrub species as well as conifer seedlings. But which is affected the most? A long-term study with group selection on the Challenge Experimental Forest in north-central California provided data that documented this effect. Another study on group-selection cutting on the Boggs Mountain State Demonstration Forest in central California quantified the effect of both shade and the roots of edge trees on conifer seedling growth. Additional analyses documented the relationship of opening size and distance from opening edge to height and diameter growth of both naturally seeded and planted ponderosa pine seedlings.

For all studies, the experimental design was completely randomized with three to six replications, called plots, in each study. Plots were rectangular and ranged from 0.1 to 0.25 acre with one or two rows of buffer (seedlings receiving similar treatment) located around sample seedlings. Statistical analysis was predominately by one- or two-way analysis of variance, with regression, simple t-tests, Bonferroni tests, mixed-model analysis, and Tukey tests also used.

Conifer seedlings selected for sampling had to have good potential of becoming harvestable trees, and chlorotic and misshapen seedlings that would be removed in the first precommercial thinning were excluded. Sampling intensity in almost all studies ranged from 25 to 35 seedlings per plot, occasionally from 15 to 40 seedlings. Stem diameter (measured at 12 in above mean groundline) and height were measured on each seedling. Needle length and foliar cover (the sum of shadows that would be cast by leaves and stems of individual species expressed as a percentage of the land surface [Daubenmire 1968]) often were quantified as well. The seedlings were periodically checked for injury from herbicides, animals, and insects.

Plant species richness (Perry 1994) was quantified when each study began, when it ended, and whenever the study area was visited. Woody and herbaceous vegetation in all studies was measured in seedling-centered, square subplots, each containing 1 milacre (0.001 acre or 43.56 ft^2) of area, with all four corners permanently marked (fig. 3). Sampling intensity almost always was five subplots per plot. Categories of species (forbs, graminoids for instance) and very abundant species were evaluated for density, foliar cover, and average dominant height (average of the three tallest stems measured from mean groundline to bud). More specifically, the number of plants in each subplot was counted, foliar cover was visually estimated to the nearest square foot, and height was measured with a graduated pole. The estimate of foliar cover was checked often by a foot-square wire frame and a graduated tape.

Figure 3—Milacre frame used to sample lesser vegetation in our studies.

The costs that we report for installing and maintaining the treatments were those of an experienced Forest Service crew that ranged from two to five workers. Costs were collected during the life of the study. No allowance for travel, equipment, or overhead was included. The cost of installing each treatment, both initially and for retreating, was based on hourly records and the prevailing wage rate for a WG-1 laborer established by the U.S. Department of Labor as of June 1993. Hence, the costs that we report have value for comparative purposes, but undoubtedly are low by current standards.

Internal moisture stress of ponderosa pine and Douglas-fir seedlings, as well as several hardwoods and shrubs, was quantified to help explain growth differences that became apparent among treatments in our study program. Xylem sap tension was measured with a Scholander pressure chamber (Scholander and others 1965) in five early studies from August 8 to August 25, in 1982 and 1984. In these studies, the conifer seedlings were about 5 years old and had been growing for 3 years after treatment.

Sampling of xylem sap tension began just before dawn and continued through late afternoon. Time and distance considerations mandated that only one replication per treatment be sampled. For this reason and because of the ever-changing amount of tension in the plants, no statistical analysis of differences among treatments was attempted. Sampling intensity was three randomly selected seedlings and shrubs of each species in each treatment. Consequently, three twigs of each species were tested in the pressure chamber at five measurement times throughout the day. Each twig was placed in a sealed plastic bag to minimize moisture change while en route to the pressure chamber. The elapsed time between cutting and placement in the chamber did not exceed 3 minutes. Every third sample was measured twice in the chamber as a check on technique and working order of the equipment. "Plant moisture stress" is expressed in atmospheres (Waring and Cleary 1967) because it is a direct reading and is familiar to foresters and biologists.

This paper has three distinct, but interacting, components: plant community development, biological influences, and operational techniques. The goal is to describe what plant species are present in young conifer plantations, how they and the communities that they represent develop, and how they can be manipulated to achieve vegetation management objectives. These interacting components can be considered as the "results" part of the paper.

Plant Community Development

After disturbance, such as from fire or site preparation, the composition of the plant community tends to be highly variable. Some species arise from root crowns or rhizomes, some from windblown seeds, and still others from dormant seeds in the soil. The distribution of plant species ranges from clumpy for some species to random for others. Number of species depends on several factors, including the kind and degree of disturbance, time since disturbance, availability of propagules, and rapidity of colonization by early invaders. Development of plants, at least for the first 10 years, is governed primarily by quality of microsite, freedom from intense competition, inherent growth rate, and herbivory.

This section documents (1) the presence and development of every plant species each year for 5 years (1976–1980) in a single study on the Challenge Experimental Forest, (2) changes in species richness within several categories of vegetation before and after 10 years in 21 study areas, and (3) development of vegetation in three differing plant communities given a wide selection of treatments.

From 1976 through 1980, every species of vegetation that was present in a small clearcutting on the Challenge Experimental Forest in north-central California was recorded and its density, foliar cover, and height were ascertained (fig. 4). Here, site quality is high and the dominant species, ponderosa pine, will average about 95 ft in height in 50 years (Powers and Oliver 1978). Site preparation was windrow and burn, which left a mostly bare mineral soil seedbed, free of vegetation above-ground. No sampling took place in or near burned windrows or in riparian zones within the sampled area.

Figure 4—Careful searching on this circular milacre subplot has identified 53 species of plants.

The first species to appear in the study area were sprouts of hardwoods and shrubs from root crowns and rhizomes as well as patches of bracken fern (*Pteridium* spp.). In late fall, conifer seeds, many seeds of annuals, and those of a few perennials blew into the area. Several thousand germinated.

After two growing seasons, thousands of plants from every regeneration strategy (Grime 1979) had become present, and those already there had grown much larger. Many grasses and forbs (annuals and perennials) also produced seeds, and species richness and population size increased greatly. Animal populations followed a similar trend, and browsing of several hardwoods, shrubs, and forbs by deer was documented. Of note, was that several of these species had new, tender, palatable foliage at this stage of development that became unpalatable the following year. More species, rapid development, and intensifying competition characterized the next three growing seasons.

In total, 71 plant species were found during the 5-year study, although no more than 62 were present during a given year (McDonald 1999). Species richness increased from 47 after 1 year to 62 after 5 years. After 5 years, average dominant height of plants in each category of vegetation ranged from 2.4 ft for graminoids (grasses and sedges) to 0.8 ft for perennials (fig. 5). Of course, this measure of height is lowered by the infusion of inherently shorter recruits. If only the tallest plants in each category were noted, then the tallest category would have been shrubs followed by conifers, graminoids, annuals, ferns, and perennials. The density of all species was 24,860 plants per acre after one growing season and increased erratically to 112,408 per acre after five seasons. Foliar cover increased each year from 950 ft^2 per acre to 17,433 ft^2 per acre after five seasons. Proportional changes in density (fig. 6) and foliar cover (fig. 7) by category each year show the developing nature of the plant community.

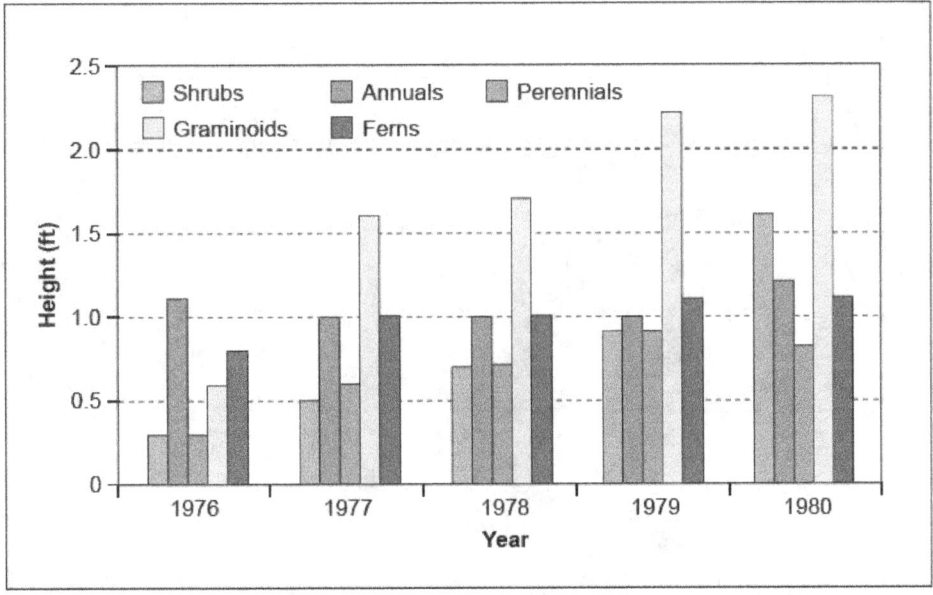

Figure 5—Height of five categories of vegetation, Challenge Experimental Forest, 1976–1980. Standard errors for shrubs ranged from 0.1 to 0.3 ft in a given year; for annual forbs, from 0.1 to 0.2; for perennial forbs, from 0.1 to 0.2; and for graminoids, from 0.2 to 0.4 ft.

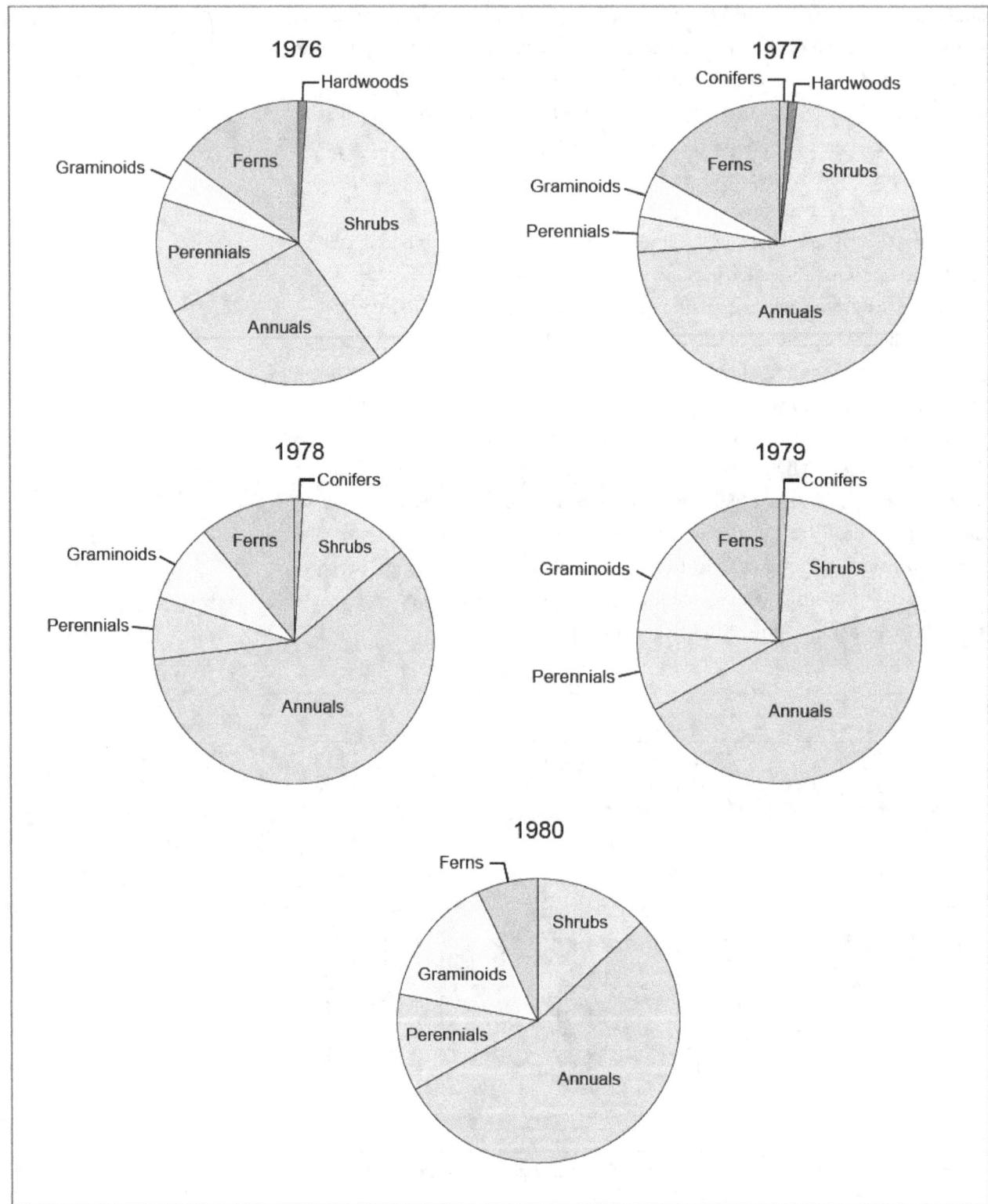

Figure 6—Proportional plant density (number per acre) for several categories of vegetation, Challenge Experimental Forest, 1976–1980.

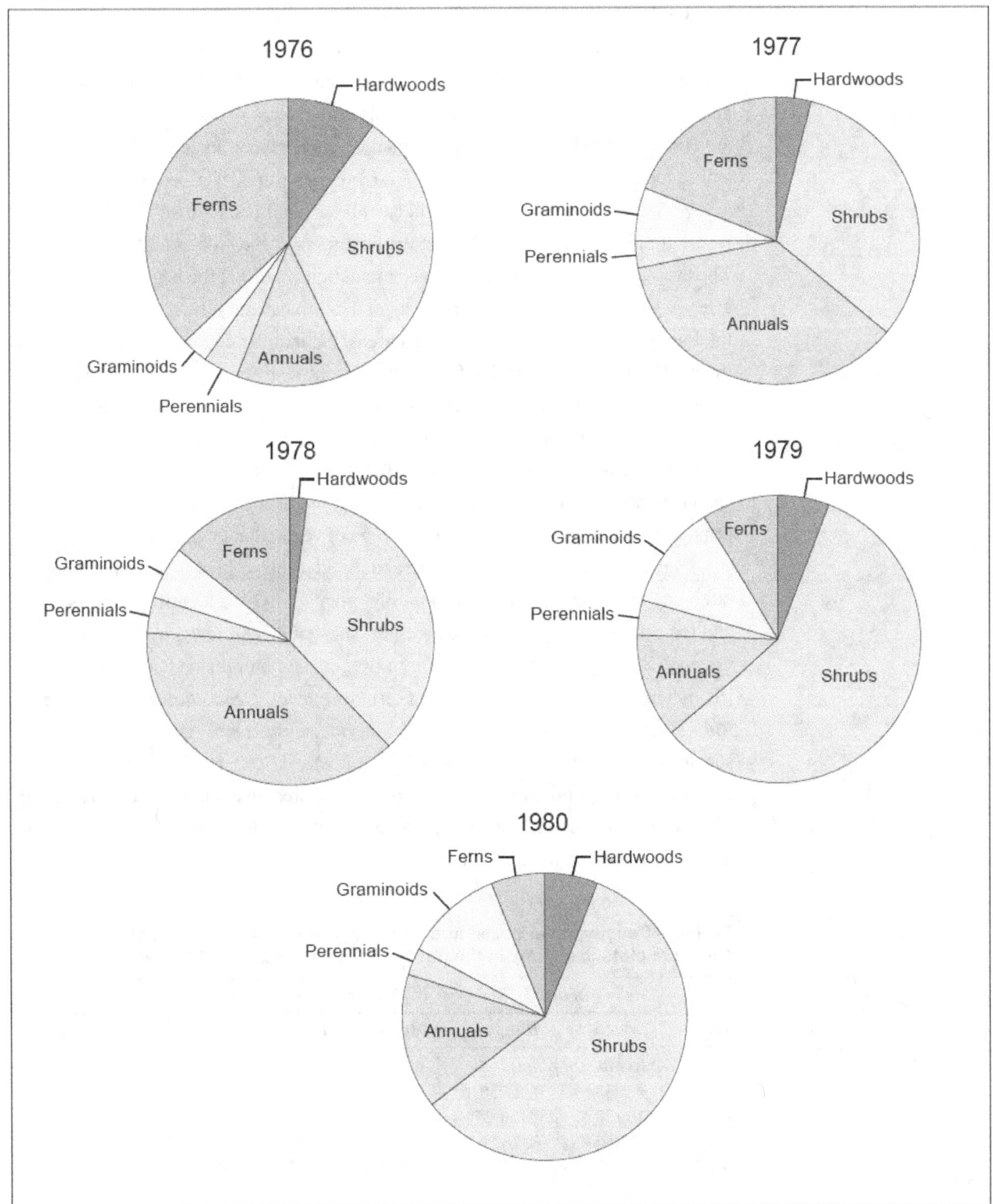

Figure 7—Proportional foliar cover (square feet per acre) for several categories of vegetation, Challenge Experimental Forest, 1976–1980.

Results from 21 study areas after 10 years portray the plant species present in young conifer plantations, how long they are present, and whether they increase or decline (McDonald and Fiddler 2006). The results also identified the plant species and genera that are most common in young plantations. Almost all of the study areas were located in conventional plantations in northern and central California whose location, site characteristics, and treatments were described in table 1.

We found 237 plant species in six categories (conifers, hardwoods, shrubs, forbs, graminoids, and ferns): 194 at the beginning of the studies and 213 at the end. The average number of species in each plantation was 23 at the beginning and 28 after 10 years. Most of the increase was in the forb category. In 12 plantations, the total number of species increased; in 8 areas, the number decreased; and in 1 area the number of species remained the same. For those areas with a species gain, the increase over 10 years was 53 percent; for those with a species loss, the decrease was 11 percent. No statistically significant difference was found between the beginning and ending plant community (p = 0.05). The range was 13 to 61 species in each plantation, with high variability and no trend of species richness related to site productivity (above to below average) or age of vegetation (5 and 10 years).

Were some core species and genera (defined as being in at least 50 percent of our study areas), common to young conifer plantations? We identified three species and ten genera. The species were greenleaf manzanita (*Arctostaphylos patula* E. Greene), Sierra gooseberry (*Ribes roezlii* Regel), and bull thistle (*Cirsium vulgare* [Savi] Ten.); the genera were *Quercus, Arctostaphylos, Ceanothus, Prunus, Ribes, Rubus, Symphoricarpos, Cirsium, Achnatherum,* and *Bromus*. Only one nonnative species in one study area (Snag) was found. It was yellow star-thistle (*Centaurea solstitialis* L.) that probably was brought into the area on a hunter's truck. Although it persevered for 10 years, it had peaked in density and foliar cover and was declining at the end of the study (table 2).

Table 2—Density, foliar cover, and height of yellow star-thistle on 15 1-milacre plots in a study in the northern Sierra Nevada, 1983–1992

Year	Density		Foliar cover		Height	
	Mean	Range	Mean	Range	Mean	Range
	Number of plants/acre		*- - - Percent - - -*		*- - - - - Feet - - - - -*	
1983	438	0–2,250	1	T^a–7	1.5	0.6–2.3
1988	10,138	250–30,250	4	T–12	1.9	0.9–3.0
1992	1,850	0–7,125	T	T	1.6	1.3–2.1

[a] T = trace.

A representative plantation in three widely differing plant communities was chosen to portray the major changes in vegetation composition over time and the magnitude of competition to conifer seedlings. These communities consisted primarily of (1) mixed shrubs; (2) mixed shrubs and graminoids; and (3) mixed shrubs, forbs, graminoids, and ferns. The number of treatments in each ranged from three to six and included herbicides, grazing, and manual release.

After 10 years, the mixed-shrub community had a smaller number of species than the other plant communities, and a range that was characterized by a lower number of plants per acre, many times more foliar cover, and taller plants (table 3). If graminoids are present, as in the mixed shrub/graminoid community, the range of plant density is huge, but the range of foliar cover and height is generally lower. If many more species are present and they are a mixture of shrubs, forbs, graminoids, and ferns, the range in density is similar to that in the mixed shrub/graminoid community, but foliar cover is much reduced, and the range in height is greater.

Table 3—Development of vegetation after a wide assortment of treatments in three differing plant communities after 10 years

Community	Number of species	Density range	Foliar cover range	Height range
		Number of plants/acre	*Square feet/acre*	*Feet*
Mixed shrubs	21	467–10,745	0–18,428	0.6–3.2
Mixed shrubs/graminoids	32	37,950–64,400	523–4,356	0.3–1.2
Shrubs, forbs, graminoids, and ferns	46	36,338–62,727	370–976	1.3–1.9

Biological Influences

Biological influences are essential for understanding the operational relationships and technologies that have been attempted and why some have been effective and some have not. This section includes information on several fundamental processes such as plant moisture stress, competition, adaptation, regeneration strategies, successional pathways, biological control, and past stand history—all of which affect the survival and growth of young conifer seedlings. The section also includes material on some complex insect-vegetation-animal interactions and on plant species replacements and exclusions—biological processes that could alleviate the need for one or more operational treatments and could be thought of as treatments themselves.

Biological influences are essential for understanding the operational relationships and technologies that have been attempted and why some have been effective and some have not.

Plant Moisture Stress

This form of internal stress was studied on ponderosa pine seedlings in two studies. In one study (Logan; McDonald and Fiddler 1995), a typical diurnal (daily) trend of internal plant moisture stress on a hot summer day indicated that seedlings treated by grubbing the entire plot had low predawn minimum stress, lower maximum stress, and lower late afternoon stress than counterparts in the other grubbing treatments (fig. 8). Conversely, seedlings in plots manually grubbed to a 4-ft radius and those in the control had to endure more and longer periods of stress. Internal moisture stress in the other study of ponderosa pine (Elk Springs; McDonald and Fiddler 1990), indicated a similar trend with seedlings in the herbicide treatment having the lowest stress and those in the control having the highest stress. Lowest to highest diurnal values for the most effective treatment in both studies ranged from 5.7 to 14.8 atmospheres, and for the least effective treatment from 8.8 to 19.3 atmospheres.

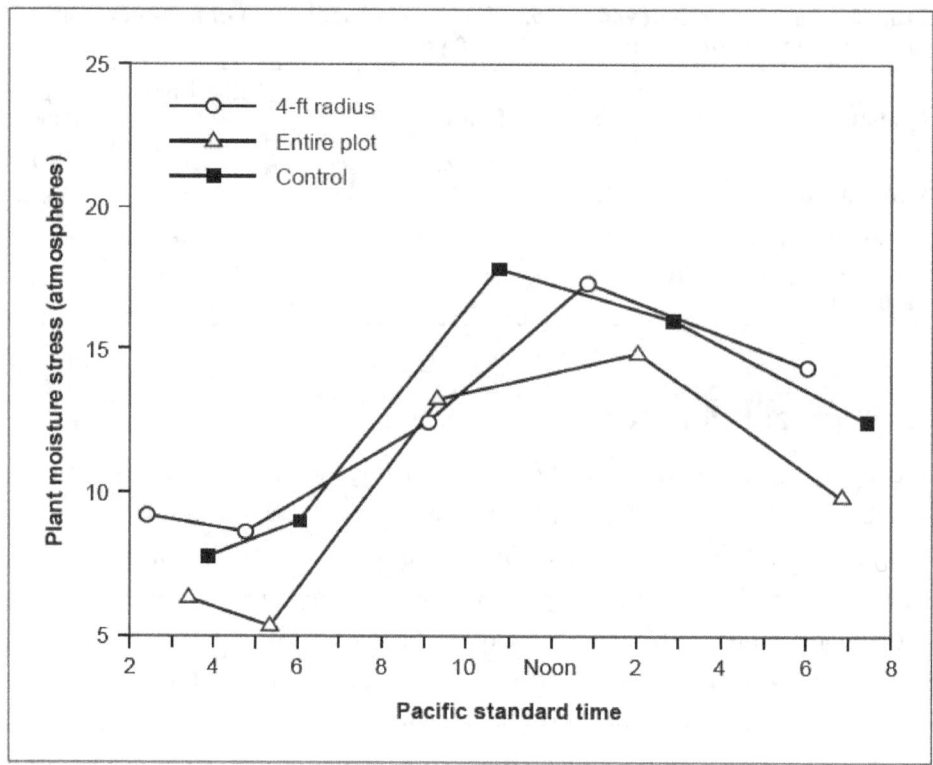

Figure 8—Trend of internal plant moisture stress of ponderosa pine seedlings in three release treatments on the Lassen National Forest, California, August 17, 1982.

For the three studies with Douglas-fir seedlings (Henry Bell, Rocky, Signal; McDonald and Fiddler 1986a, 1996, 1999b), the lowest internal moisture stress values generally occurred in seedlings in treatments that effectively targeted the most vigorous competing species. Seedlings in plots treated with 2,4-D, cut and spray with Garlon 3A, and grubbing the entire plot had the lowest internal moisture stress. The highest stress occurred in seedlings on plots that had a 2-ft grubbed radius or in the untreated control. Lowest to highest diurnal values for the most biologically effective treatment in the three studies ranged from 4.5 to 22 atmospheres, and for the least effective treatment from 13 to 28 atmospheres.

Internal moisture stress of root-crown sprouts of tanoak (*Lithocarpus densiflorus* [Hook. & Arn.] Rehd.) was evaluated in two studies in northwestern California (Rocky, Signal; McDonald and Fiddler 1996, 1999b), and, as for Douglas-fir seedlings, was found to be lower in treatments that targeted the species that were the most competitive to them. Tanoak sprouts in plots treated with Garlon 4 or a tank mix of Garlon 4 and 2,4-D had the lowest values, and those in the control and in plots grubbed to a 5-ft radius one time had the highest values. Lowest to highest diurnal values for tanoak in the most effective treatment (herbicides) in the two studies ranged from 4 to 8 atmospheres, and for the least effective treatments (grubbing, control) from 7 to 18 atmospheres.

Internal moisture stress was evaluated in two species of *Ceanothus*: deerbrush (*C. integerrimus* Hook. & Arn.) and snowbrush (*C. velutinus* Hook. var. *velutinus*). For deerbrush, it was lowest in plots where the entire area was manually released and highest in plots that were manually grubbed to a 4-ft radius. Lowest to highest values for the most effective treatment were 13.5 to 32.5 atmospheres, and for the least effective treatment from 32.5 to 42.7 atmospheres (Henry Bell; McDonald and Fiddler 1986a). For snowbrush, internal moisture stress was lowest in plots where the entire area was grubbed and highest in those grubbed to a 4-ft radius (Logan; McDonald and Fiddler 1995). Lowest to highest values ranged from 6.3 to 16.3 atmospheres in plots where the entire area was grubbed to 8.0 to 18.7 atmospheres in plots grubbed to a 4-ft radius.

We also quantified internal moisture stress in two species of manzanita: greenleaf manzanita and hairy manzanita (*A. columbiana* Piper). For greenleaf manzanita, internal moisture stress was lowest in plots where the entire area was manually grubbed and highest in plots grubbed to a 4-ft radius. Stress values ranged from 6.4 to 17.0 atmospheres in entire-area-treated plots and from 10.2 to 23.8 atmospheres in radius-grubbed plots (Logan; McDonald and Fiddler 1995). For hairy manzanita, internal moisture stress was lowest in plots treated with 2,4-D

Competition is a complex ecological process with many biological, environmental, and proximity factors that interact when plants grow together over time. Competition for critical environmental resources such as light, water, and nutrients, which are necessary for photosynthesis and respiration, is primarily responsible for the negative interaction between conifer seedlings and other vegetation.

where values ranged from 3.5 to 9.2 atmospheres, and highest in plots treated by a 5-ft radius one time (Signal; McDonald and Fiddler 1999b). Here values ranged from 7.5 to 22 atmospheres.

Competition

Competition is a complex ecological process with many biological, environmental, and proximity factors that interact when plants grow together over time. Competition for critical environmental resources such as light, water, and nutrients, which are necessary for photosynthesis and respiration, is primarily responsible for the negative interaction between conifer seedlings and other vegetation. Over 200 studies in the United States have demonstrated that small increases in the density or biomass of competing vegetation significantly lower conifer seedling survival and growth (Stewart and others 1984).

Given the long hot summers typical of most of California, it stands to reason that competition to conifer seedlings involves adequate soil moisture, and this means that the seat of early competition is belowground at the fine-root level. A likely scenario follows: In the absence of competition, the roots of young conifer seedlings extend vertically at the maximum rate possible. They increase in width and length, number of root tips, and in moisture absorption capacity. By increasing the volume of soil exploited, they increase the amount of water and nutrients available for rapid growth. The resources stored in or acquired by the root system lead to production of more aboveground biomass and more carbohydrates. This in turn fuels additional growth both above and belowground in a manner that accelerates each year. But competing shrubs and grasses, if present, characteristically begin root expansion and soil exploitation earlier in the growing season and in greater amounts than the conifer seedlings and capture the bulk of available site resources. The contrast between new pines and grass is striking. Based on measurements of several thousand seedlings from federal, state, and private nurseries, a typical 1-year-old ponderosa pine seedling had a total root length of about 78 in (McDonald and Fiddler 1989). A single wild oat plant excavated 80 days after emergence had developed a root system that totaled over 50 mi in length (Radosevich and Holt 1984). The lack of initial resources stresses the conifer seedling by causing decreased root expansion, less resource collection, poor growth, and, in many instances, death. Even if the seedling survives, losses in growth are seldom made up.

Plainly, it is not just competition but **early** competition that has the most impact on the survival and growth of planted conifer seedlings. In a study with California white fir seedlings near Mount Shasta, California (Stephens Pass A), treatments were applied at different times and lasted for different durations in an effort to demonstrate the effect of early release (McDonald and Fiddler 2001A). When seedlings were released each year 4 to 6 years after planting, they had statistically smaller average diameters than if released each year for only the first 3 years. Furthermore, the mean diameter of seedlings with the delayed release did not differ statistically ($p < 0.05$) from seedlings in the untreated control.

In southwest Oregon, Douglas-fir seedlings were planted in treated and untreated plots (control) where competing vegetation was primarily rapidly growing sprouts of canyon live oak (*Quercus chrysolepis* Liebm.) and greenleaf manzanita. After just one growing season, the negative effect of the resprouting shrubs could be seen. After three seasons, the growth of Douglas-fir seedlings planted in treated (slashed) 3-year-old sprouts was just as poor as those planted in the untreated control (Tesch and Hobbs 1989), indicating the power of the shrubs to recover and capture site resources. After five growing seasons, excavation showed that seedlings in the control and slashed areas had produced virtually no new roots and had retained the same shape of root system as when planted. But root biomass of the essentially free-to-grow seedlings was 9 times that of seedlings planted after slashing and 22 times that of seedlings in the control (Tesch 1991).

In a study in northern California, biomass accumulation of 1-year-old greenleaf manzanita plants on good site was almost 60 times that of ponderosa pine seedlings (Radosevich 1984). After the third growing season, reductions of 80 to 90 percent in pine growth were noted from shrub proportions of 50 percent or more. Reducing manzanita density by 75 percent did not free pine seedlings for adequate growth because rapid regrowth by the remaining 25 percent soon equaled the competitive effect of that removed.

On the lower slopes of Mount Shasta in northern California, a long-term study on a poor site exemplified the effect of competition. Here, ponderosa pine seedling growth was quantified in replicated plots containing various densities of aggressive woody shrubs that ranged from none to heavy (McDonald and Abbott 1997). From 1966 through 1992, the regressed value of pines without competition was 25.0 ft tall; with light competition, 17.5 ft tall; with medium competition, 12.5 ft tall; and with heavy competition, 7.0 ft tall. Best-fit regression of these data is shown (fig. 9). Furthermore, the slope of the curves indicated that the differences in growth were accelerating. Similar findings were found for average foliar cover (fig. 10) and crown volume as well.

> **It is not just competition but early competition that has the most impact on the survival and growth of planted conifer seedlings.**

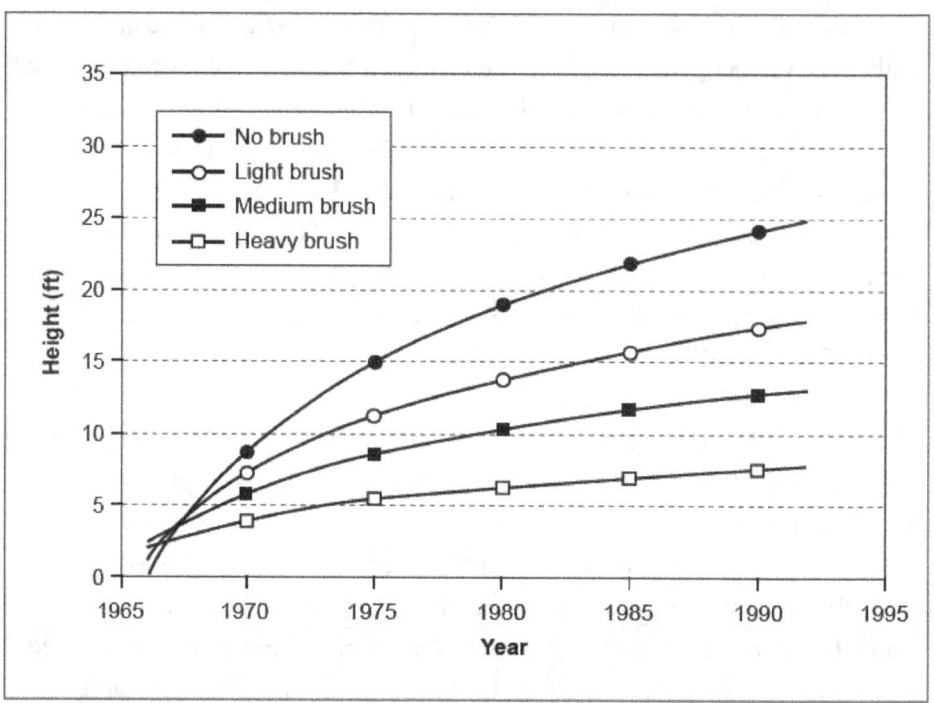

Figure 9—Relationship of ponderosa pine height to shrub density category, Mount Shasta brushfields, 1966–1992.

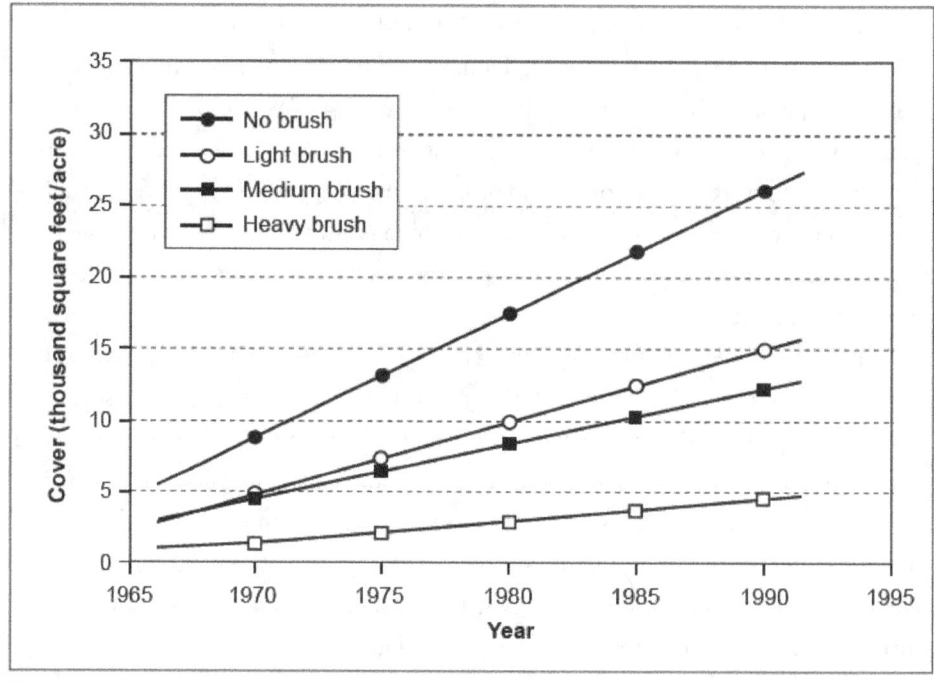

Figure 10—Relationship of ponderosa pine foliar cover to shrub density category, Mount Shasta brushfields, 1966–1992.

Adaptation, Regeneration Strategies, and Successional Pathways

The one "truth" that approaches absolute in vegetation management is that Mother Nature abhors bare ground. Moreover, almost all plant species in summer-dry California have a strategy for taking advantage of disturbance with rapid early growth. Success in completing the life cycle accrues to those plants that can get to, and stay in, a zone of adequate soil moisture. Even after good site preparation, the number of pioneering species and the number of plants are impressive. Densities of 10,000 plants per acre, 1 year after site preparation are conservative. A few years later, a density of more than 100,000 plants per acre is common if grasses and forbs constitute the majority of invaders. Adaptation, regeneration strategies, and successional pathways are processes that plant species employ to practically guarantee that bare ground does not stay bare for long.

Adaptation—

Through natural selection over millions of years, competing plant species tend to be well adapted to the harsh environment of the new plantation, particularly in the summer, which often is characterized by low precipitation, high temperatures, low relative humidity, and searing winds. Many shrubs, for example, have a host of morphological and physiological adaptations that allow them to prosper in a broad range of microsites, some of which are environmentally harsh for establishing conifer species. And the harsher the site, the better adapted are the shrubs relative to the conifers. Indeed, "shrubs exemplify more than any other kinds of plants, the great plasticity that has been largely responsible for the outstanding evolutionary success achieved by flowering plants" (Stebbins 1972).

Sunken stomates, thick cell walls, large root systems, crown architecture and smooth bark to facilitate stem flow, and capability to fix carbon at relatively high levels of moisture stress are but a few of the adaptations characteristic of many shrub species. Capability to limit the loss of moisture and ability to use that which is available efficiently (McDonald 1982) is an extremely valuable adaptation. Ability to limit respiration when internal moisture levels are low and temperatures are high is an outstanding adaptation that permits use of nearly all available moisture without penalty of wilting or depletion of energy reserves (Mooney and Dunn 1970). Another physiological adaptation of many shrubs and some trees is the ability to consume most of the available soil moisture early in the spring to attain maximum photosynthesis at the expense of reduced photosynthesis and growth later in the season. This hoarding of moisture also limits the survival and growth of competing species.

Through natural selection over millions of years, competing plant species tend to be well adapted to the harsh environment of the new plantation, particularly in the summer, which often is characterized by low precipitation, high temperatures, low relative humidity, and searing winds.

Two widespread shrub species that have many of the above adaptations are deerbrush and greenleaf manzanita, but which of them best uses these adaptations to gain an early growth advantage? Such information is worthwhile in its own right and also is useful for comparison to the growth rates of conifer seedlings. Growth of deerbrush and greenleaf manzanita was compared in a replicated side-by-side study in northern California (McDonald and others 1998). Seed was gathered from a local source, grown in a nursery for several months, and outplanted in spring 1992 on a cleared site of high quality. The shrub seedlings were 2 to 4 in tall when outplanted. Number of stems per plant, crown diameter, height of tallest stem, and phenology (leaf development, onset and duration of flowering, seed production and dissemination, leaf fall) were recorded at various times throughout the year from 1992 through 1995.

The development of deerbrush and greenleaf manzanita was similar in some respects and different in others. Both species sustained moderate first-year mortality (17 versus 11 percent, respectively), no subsequent mortality, multiple stems on most plants (5.6 versus 3.6 stems per plant), maintained the initial proportion of plants with multiple stems (89 versus 76 percent), and grew rapidly. For differences between species, deerbrush developed a clump of stems the first growing season and greenleaf manzanita the second. By the end of the second growing season, deerbrush had produced statistically more stems per plant, was taller, and had wider crowns than greenleaf manzanita (table 4). Deerbrush also began to produce flowers and seed during the third growing season, but manzanita did not do so during the 4-year study.

Table 4—Comparison of average height and crown width between deerbrush and greenleaf manzanita plants, Mount Shasta Ranger District, 1992–1995

Species	Year	Height	Probability[a]	Crown width	Probability
		Inches		*Inches*	
Deerbrush	1992	5.4		5.6	
Manzanita		4.9	0.3700	4.3	0.0403
Deerbrush	1993	18.8		29.4	
Manzanita		12.2	.0001	10.9	.0001
Deerbrush	1994	32.0		42.9	
Manzanita		18.5	.0001	18.8	.0001
Deerbrush	1995	40.4		51.5	
Manzanita		24.9	.0001	27.0	.0001

[a] Based on a two-way analysis of variance.

These differences suggest that deerbrush is the more competitive species, at least in early years. More stems per clump means a wider clump, and this, plus greater height, allows occupation of a larger area sooner than rival greenleaf manzanita. And being able to produce seed soon after disturbance enables at least some new plants to occupy favorable microsites that quickly become unavailable. Grasses are equally well adapted (Logan 1982), especially belowground where huge masses of fine roots efficiently capture soil moisture (Trappe 1981). Forbs also can furnish strong competition to young conifer seedlings because they often consist of many species that together occupy all available niches above and belowground for an extended period (McDonald and others 1994a).

Regeneration strategies—
Conifer plantations characteristically occupy areas that have been severely disturbed by timber harvest and site preparation. Here, slash has been windrowed and perhaps burned, and most remaining vegetation has been uprooted and removed. Soil surfaces in these areas often are almost bare and temporarily devoid of most plants and animals. While harsh aboveground, the environment belowground is benign. In the spring following disturbance, available resources are high because large quantities of organic material have been incorporated into the soil and large quantities of moisture are absorbed by it. Warm temperatures and plentiful moisture cause a rapid buildup of micro-organisms that decompose organic material and liberate nutrients. In this rapidly changing and somewhat unstable environment, plant species compete effectively by using different strategies of reproduction and development.

Regeneration strategies fall into two main groups: those that involve the reproductive potential of plants, and those that affect plant growth. Strategies that affect reproductive potential include windblown seeds, seed banks, and banks of persistent seedlings (Grime 1979). Strategies that affect growth potential include vegetative expansion aboveground and vegetative elongation belowground.

The relatively bare ground of new conifer plantations serves as a near-perfect medium for colonization by wind-dispersed seeds from species having small seeds with large wings, plumes, or pappus. Both woody and herbaceous species regenerate with this strategy. They often produce huge amounts of seed that are carried long distances by wind and effectively saturate an area. Herbaceous species of the family Compositae are common windblown invaders, as are plant species from the genera *Cirsium, Madia, Epilobium, Stephanomeria, Hypochoeris*, and *Senecio*. Small seeds often mean meager reserves of stored food, short viability timespans, and low competitive capability of the seedlings. Species with wind-dispersed seeds often circumvent these shortcomings with biennial cycles. Their seeds blow in on the wind in fall, germinate after the fall rains, punch a taproot into the soil for a few inches, and overwinter as short, inconspicuous plants. They then resume growth in the spring when soil temperatures are still cold enough to inhibit root growth of conifer seedlings. Fueled by the underutilized resources in the plantation area, and with their photosynthetic apparatus already in place, these plants bolt, grow vigorously, and complete their life cycles. A good example is bull thistle, where in a new plantation on a good site in the northern Sierra Nevada of California, peak density was 34,000 seedlings per acre (McDonald and Tappeiner 1986). In another study on the Tahoe National Forest in northern California (Snag), the thistle population neared 60,000 plants per acre and the thistledown (winged seeds) was so great that it covered the plantation in places to the point that lower plants could not be seen. In both studies, pine survival was lowered to the point that the studies were jeopardized. Populations of windblown species usually peak after 2 to 4 years, but while present, constitute a formidable drain on site resources.

Plant species with the seed-bank reproductive strategy generally produce seeds that are incorporated in the litter and soil in a dormant condition for at least 1 year. These seeds almost always are small and have dormant embryos and hard seed coats that prevent imbibition of water. Length of time in the soil may range from a few years to centuries. Families of plants in young plantations include Compositae, Cruciferae, Ericaceae, Gramineae, Polygonaceae, Ranunculaceae, Rosaceae, and Scrophulariaceae. The number of seeds in a persistent seed bank may differ greatly for a given species, but, in general, is largest after a bumper seed crop. A general trend is for seed density and viability to decrease with soil depth. Because nature does not like to risk the entire seed crop in the soil, polymorphism in germination requirements is an attribute of the seed of most species with this reproductive strategy. Thus only some seeds germinate at a given time and a reservoir of seeds remains intact.

A study at the base of Mount Shasta on the Shasta-Trinity National Forest in a converted brushfield (McBride) was notable for the endless supply of new greenleaf manzanita seedlings from the seed bank in the soil. Thousands of plants per acre were present initially, with manual grubbing facilitating a new crop of seedlings each year for 3 successive years (McDonald and Fiddler 2001a).

Plants of shade-tolerant species, which often are lower in stature than vegetative associates, are found in the understory in the seedling-bank reproductive strategy and accumulate for many years. Shoot growth is slow or even negative because of dieback, but root systems expand slowly and may develop rudimentary burls that serve as food-storage organs (McDonald and Tappeiner 1986). Surviving for long periods under unfavorable circumstances ensures that the potential for regeneration is maintained until gaps in the overstory are created, or until the entire overstory is removed by senescence, insects, disease, windfall, fires, or harvest. After release, the seedlings take advantage of the additional site resources, especially light, and grow at a faster rate.

Tanoak provides a good example of the seedling-bank regenerative strategy. This species regenerates from seed, root-crown sprouts, and seedling sprouts. Seedlings from acorns almost always die back to the root crown, then sprout and become seedling sprouts (stems arising from stumps less than 1 inch in diameter at ground line). Capability to sprout had been observed to occur within 7 days of emergence on hundreds of tanoak seedlings in a large plantation (McDonald 1978). Detailed examination of growth rings above and below the burl, which form at about age 3, revealed that tanoak seedling sprouts may be up to 62 years old and less than 85 in tall. Sprouts have died back and sprouted several times by this age, and stem age just below the burl is much greater than sprout age above the burl (Tappeiner and McDonald 1984). The number of sprouts per stump ranges from 2 to 14, and the number of seedling sprouts may exceed 10,000 per acre. After release by cutting or burning, the seedling sprouts die back, sprout, and grow vigorously, fueled by intake from the root system and augmented by food reserves stored in the burl.

Seedling sprouts of several hardwoods and shade-tolerant shrubs of the genera *Prunus* and *Chrysolepis* were present in several of our studies. Their characteristically slow development left them vulnerable to rapidly growing root-crown sprouts of their own and other species, and most were relegated once again to the understory.

The above regeneration strategies concern seed and equally importantly, its dissemination. Wind and the feet, feathers, fur, and digestive tracts of animals are important for spreading the species to new, sometimes more advantageous, locations. The huge seed crops typical of many shrubs, forbs, graminoids, and hardwoods in young plantations not only sustain the species, but also the animal disseminators. Grinnell (1936) said it well: "It is not extravagance, but good investment for the oaks to provide subsistence for a continuing population of animal associates."

Another regeneration strategy of plants in recently disturbed areas is rapid expansion aboveground. It is accomplished almost entirely by root-crown sprouts of hardwood trees and woody shrubs that originate from dormant buds on burls located at or just belowground line. Many species of many genera have this strategy including *Arbutus*, *Arctostaphylos*, *Ceanothus*, *Lithocarpus*, *Quercus*, and *Rhamnus*. These species occupy an environment where wildfire is common and where the conifer trees are killed outright, but the hardwood trees and woody shrubs are killed only to ground line.

Root-crown sprouts are often thought of as being "instant reproduction" because of their abundance and rapid growth. Number of sprouts per stump can differ from several score to 1,400 on one large tanoak stump (Tappeiner and others 1990). Enriched by the food reserves and extensive root system of parent plants, root-crown sprouts grow as much as 5 ft in height in one growing season. After three growing seasons in northwestern California, sprouts of bigleaf maple (*Acer macrophyllum* Pursh) were 12.8 ft tall, those of Pacific madrone (*Arbutus menziesii* Pursh) were 10.1 ft tall, and sprouts of tanoak were 6.8 ft tall (Roy 1955). Rapid expansion continues. On a good site in north-central California, average 10-year clump height and width in a clearcutting were Pacific madrone 20 ft tall, 10-ft wide; tanoak 19 ft tall, 10 ft wide; and California black oak 20 ft tall, and 10 ft wide (McDonald and Tappeiner 2002).

Woody shrubs also have capability for sustained rapid growth. In our study near the Pacific Ocean on a good site (Signal), snowbrush (*Ceanothus velutinus* Hook. var. *hookeri* M. Johnston) and blue blossom (*Ceanothus thyrsiflorus* Eschsch.) were over 30 ft tall after 10 years of growth (McDonald and Fiddler 1999b). A much less vigorous component of the rapid expansion above-ground strategy is from trailing stems that root freely. Such plant species as mahala mat (*Ceanothus prostratus* Benth.) and creeping snowberry (*Symphoricarpos mollis* Nutt.) were found in our study on the Plumas National Forest in the northern Sierra Nevada (Deans) (McDonald and Fiddler 2007).

An outstanding reproductive strategy, particularly on poor sites, is vegetative expansion belowground by rhizomes and root sprouts. The below-ground location and attachment to a food source practically guarantees a low risk of mortality and successful establishment of the offspring. Areas with already established vegetation, deep litter layers, or where establishment from seed is difficult because of chronic destruction or consumption are other conditions where this strategy serves its species well. Representative species in many of our study areas were from the genera *Apocynum*, *Aster*, *Convolvulus*, *Gaultheria*, *Nama*, *Pteridium*, *Rubus*, and *Vaccinium*. Species from these genera often form dense patches and suppress the regeneration and growth of other species.

Species that propagate from root sprouts were not common in our study areas with one exception—Sierra plum (*Prunus subcordata* Benth.). This shrub also produces intermittent crops of large seeds in nutritious fruits, and may occasionally reproduce from rootcrowns. In the long-term study on the lower slopes of Mount Shasta, not a single new seedling of Sierra plum was found (McDonald and Abbott

An outstanding reproductive strategy, particularly on poor sites, is vegetative expansion belowground by rhizomes and root sprouts. The below-ground location and attachment to a food source practically guarantees a low risk of mortality and successful establishment of the offspring.

1997). Apparently all seed was consumed by herbivores. Over the 1966–1992 study, sprout density, foliar cover, and volume generally declined and height increased marginally. Height growth was beset by periods of dieback and resprouting and in general was less than other shrub species.

Another species with multiple regenerative strategies is bearclover (*Chamaebatia foliolosa* Benth.). It sprouts from the rootcrown, produces rhizomes, forms scores of flowers, and, at least in one instance (McDonald and Fiddler 1999c), sends up root sprouts from deep in the soil. In a new plantation in north-central California, bearclover produced more than 224,000 stems and 24,800 ft^2 of foliar cover per acre when less than 1 ft tall. Unlike Sierra plum, which often resides in the understory of taller trees and shrubs, bearclover dominates over thousands of acres of open and semiopen forest land in northern California, and has withstood a wide variety of treatments aimed at its control (McDonald and others 2004).

Successional pathways—
Of the two classical types of plant succession, it is secondary succession that is operative in young conifer plantations because it involves revegetation after disturbance. Secondary succession is a complex phenomenon that involves the regenerative strategies and the dispersal efficiencies of plants and their capability to progressively modify the soil and microenvironment. Odom (1969) suggested that succession is an orderly process of community development that is reasonably directional and therefore predictable. Knowledge of succession is important because vegetation management often sets an initial point (bare ground) through site preparation, and imposes a narrow range of environmental conditions that lead to a particular (often desired) plant community.

Connell and Slatyer (1977) described three mechanisms that govern succession in the plant community. Species with a "facilitation" mechanism require earlier species to modify the environment for their entry and growth. Facilitators can colonize only after suitable changes in the microenvironment. Species having the "tolerance" mechanism can become established in locales having inhibiting chemicals or lower levels of site resources. These species generate a predictable successional sequence in which later colonizers invade and grow to maturity in the presence of those that preceded them. The "inhibition" mechanism, finally, operates where all species, even the earliest, resist invasion by competitors. The first occupants preempt space and exclude or inhibit later colonists. Later colonizers become established and reach maturity only after the first become damaged or die. Morris and Wood (1989) found that pioneer species can both facilitate and inhibit subsequent invaders.

> **Knowledge of succession is important because vegetation management often sets an initial point (bare ground) through site preparation, and imposes a narrow range of environmental conditions that lead to a particular (often desired) plant community.**

Plant succession in the vast majority of the study areas in our *National Study on Vegetation Management in California* followed a general pattern. The first species to appear were those that escaped death from site preparation and arose from rhizomes or root crown sprouts. The next colonizers came from buried seeds in the soil followed by seed from a few species that blew in on the wind or were carried into the area by animals. Within a year or two, almost all species were producing at least some seed, and together with new arrivals from the soil and wind, constituted a dynamic and rapidly expanding population dedicated to capturing site resources and completing life cycles.

Biological Control and Exclusion

Biological control is defined as the use of living organisms to lower plant pest populations to the point where the pests are no longer management or economic problems.

If a desired plant species naturally replaces an undesired plant species, the desired species in effect becomes a treatment and the cost of manipulation and control are either eliminated or much reduced. This process often is termed biological control and is defined as the use of living organisms to lower plant pest populations to the point where the pests are no longer management or economic problems. Besides animals and micro-organisms, biological control agents can be other plants that are either parasitic, competitive, or allelopathic (Rosenthal and others 1985). Not only does biological control have the advantage of cost, it also has a social attribute. In sensitive areas, this means of weed control may be the only method applicable.

Short, shallow-rooted forbs, that consume only a small amount of soil moisture are ideal candidates for biological control if they limit more aggressive shrubs. In a study on the Lassen National Forest on a good site (Logan) (McDonald and Fiddler 1995) and another on the Tahoe National Forest on a poor site (McDonald 2003), wooly nama (*Nama lobbii* A. Gray), which is a low, shallow-rooted forb, quickly became established on plots where most of the competing vegetation had been eliminated by site preparation. This species prefers bright sunlight and declines in shade. It becomes present soon after site preparation, spreads rapidly, and forms dense masses of vegetation. This forb suppresses germination of dormant shrub seeds in the soil for at least 5 years or until shaded out by rapidly growing pines. Smooth cat's ear (*Hypochaeris glabra* L.), hairy cat's ear (*H. radicata* L.), and prickly lettuce (*Lactuca serriola* L.) are other shallow-rooted forbs that invade recently disturbed areas in large numbers and preempt site resources (McDonald and Fiddler 1993a).

Another example of plant species exclusion took place in a converted brushfield on a medium-poor site in the southern Cascade Mountains northeast of McCloud, California. One of the three dominant shrub species was bitter cherry (*Prunus emarginata* [Hook.] Walp.) that was 4 to 5 ft tall before the site was prepared by windrowing and burning (McDonald and Fiddler 1997b). Following site preparation, the density of bitter cherry decreased steadily from 487 plants per acre after 1 year to zero plants per acre after 5 years. Number of species increased from 9 to 17 during the 10-year study, and three other shrubs had large increases in density and foliar cover. Competition-induced drought is the likely cause for the exclusion of bitter cherry.

The long-term study on the lower slopes of Mount Shasta (McDonald and Abbott 1997) provides a good example of a shrub-pine seedling-graminoid competitive interaction and biological control. Five years after planting of the pines, needlegrass (*Achnatherum nelsonii* [Scribner] Barkworth ssp. *dorei* [Barkworth & J. Maze] Barkworth) began to invade the area. Needlegrass density was inversely related to shrub density: the more the shrubs, the less the grass. Of importance was that on the plots where the shrubs were eliminated, grass density was high, and no new shrubs were found in spite of the virtual certainty that more seeds were buried in the soil and more were carried in from nearby areas by birds and animals.

Interference by the needlegrass prevented germination of shrub seeds and the grass excluded the shrubs. Because the grass became established after the pines, and the grass roots were not as deep as those of the pines, it constituted only minor competition to them. Eventually, the pines almost eliminated the grass (table 5).

Table 5—Relation of needlegrass density to shrub-density class 18 and 31 years after planting in a ponderosa pine plantation near Mount Shasta, California

Shrub density class	Age (years)	
	18	**31**
	Number of plants/acre	
None	50,000	540
Light	17,600	0
Medium	8,200	0
Heavy	533	0

Another aspect of replacement vegetation for biological control of undesirable vegetation involves the introduction of beneficial plant species that are not native to the area. These species often have the attribute of being preferred by domestic grazing animals like cattle and sheep. A concern is that they replace native plant species, especially smaller forbs and grasses. In one of our studies on the Tahoe National Forest (Cattle II), we hand seeded Potomac orchardgrass (*Dactylis glomerata* L.) and pubescent wheatgrass (*Agropyron trichophorum* [Link] Richter) and quantified their density, foliar cover and height along with that of manzanita (*Arctostaphylos* spp.), other shrubs, and grasses in a ponderosa pine plantation grazed by cattle (McDonald and Fiddler 1999a, 2002).

In general, the introduced grasses, along with the native needlegrass, became established in a wide range of niches including sun and shade and grazed and ungrazed, and grew well irrespective of the kind and amount of other vegetation. They also benefited from grazing and had higher density in grazed plots than in ungrazed plots. As a whole, the effect of the introduced grasses was minor, although slightly beneficial because of the weight gain of the cattle. They did not appear to replace native plant species nor were they excluded by them. Indeed, a total of 34 plant species was found in the study area over an 11-year period. Other investigators (Eissenstat and Mitchell 1983, Krueger 1983) have found similar results in grazing studies in the Western United States.

Vegetation managers occasionally try to biologically control a vigorous native species by introducing a nonnative species. On the Stanislaus National Forest, a study (Grapevine) was designed to specifically test the effect of nonnative annual ryegrass (*Lolium multiflorum* L.) on the regrowth of native bearclover. The study area burned in a wildfire in late summer 1987 and was seeded to annual ryegrass that fall. A vigorous stand of grass became established in 1988, and a myriad of seed was produced. Each of these seeds produced a plant in 1989, and sampling revealed a density of over 10 million per acre by that fall. Thus bearclover had to sprout and regrow in an environment characterized by a very high level of established competition.

Results from the study plots in fall 1992 showed a dramatic decrease in number of stems of both bearclover and ryegrass (table 6). Although both species maintained their initial height values, the density of grass actually fell below that of bearclover in 1992, indicating that the grass population was being stressed by the bearclover. Subsequent visits to the study site indicated the total domination of bearclover and its virtual immunity to competition from this vigorous grass. Unfortunately the study area was burned by a forest fire in 1996.

Table 6—Average stem density and height of bearclover and annual ryegrass (*Lolium multiflorum* L.), Stanislaus National Forest, 1989 and 1992

	Bearclover				Ryegrass			
	Density		Height		Density		Height	
Year	Mean	SE[a]	Mean	SE	Mean	SE	Mean	SE
	Number of stems/acre		- - - *Feet* - - -		*Number of stems/acre*		- - *Feet* - -	
1989	339,900	12,200	0.8	0.1	10,489,000	805,000	1.6	0.1
1992	9,867	1,555	.9	.1	9,133	1,711	1.6	.1

[a] SE = standard error.

Not only can individual species of replacement vegetation influence future plant community composition and dynamics, but the sheer amount of vegetation from other categories may constitute replacement as well. In one of our studies (Harrison Gulch) on the Shasta-Trinity National Forest, for example, the number of forb, fern, and grass species and their density increased very rapidly in all treatments and in the untreated control (McDonald and Fiddler 1997). After 10 years, species numbered 46 and average density 217,800 plants per acre in the control and 177,105 per acre in the most effective treatment (5-ft radius, grubbed three times). It is likely that competition from the forbs, ferns, and grasses interfered with the establishment of highly competitive shrubs from seeds in the soil.

Insect-Vegetation-Animal Interactions

Vegetation managers need to be watchful for complex vegetation-insect and insect-vegetation-animal interactions that may harm their plantations. One interaction took place on the lower slopes of Mount Shasta where it relates to shrub density, pine seedling height, and insect damage. The setting was the long-term study mentioned earlier involving plots manipulated to create the range of no shrubs to heavy shrubs (McDonald and Abbott 1997). Insect damage to the pines, principally by the gouty pitch midge (*Cecidoymia piniinopis* Osten Sacken) (Bedard and others 1989), and specifically death of terminal shoots, did not become serious until the pines were about 8 years old and continued for another 10 years. More than five times as many terminal shoots were killed on pines in heavy shrubs as in light shrubs during this timespan. The general trend was an increasing number of dead terminals with increasing shrub density (fig. 11). Apparently the shrub environment is, or perhaps the weaker trees in the shrub environment are, favorable to the insects. After the trees reached a height of 12 ft, damage to terminals lessened appreciably. Damage to lateral shoots by the pine needle-sheath miner (*Zelleria haimbachi* Busch) (Stevens 1959) followed the same general trend with less damage above 12 ft. By slowing pine height growth, the shrubs held the trees below this height.

Figure 11—Insects have killed the terminal shoot of this pine seedling many times.

The insects then attacked the trees, deformed them, and together with the shrubs, continued to hold the trees to a size where they are attacked repeatedly. The insect and the shrubs together did more damage to the pines than either alone.

Another interaction, again on the west-facing slope of Mount Shasta, took place in a large brushy compartment that was treated with herbicide to promote broadcast burning. Several years after planting ponderosa pine seedlings, copious amounts of shrubs and grasses that emerged were again treated with an herbicide. The shrubs were affected greatly, the grasses were not. Pocket gophers were attracted to the grassy environment, and a wingless grasshopper (*Bradynotes obesa opima* Scudder) (Furniss and Carolin 1977) soon became epidemic. The shift from shrubs to grass and corresponding increase in pocket gophers and grasshoppers caused the loss of most of the pine seedlings (McDonald and Tappeiner 1986).

Past Stand History

An enduring theme in vegetation management is the study of human alteration of the forest. This alteration often has the goal of modifying the forest to purposeful ends, but sometimes it is not achieved because of events that happened in the past. Past stand events are a major factor governing which species occur at what locations in the landscape. If greenleaf manzanita, for example, was present before it was replaced by conifer trees, its seed remains in the soil, and it will be present again in large numbers after disturbance. A good example of this occurred in northern California where the brushy site was prepared by windrow and burn. One year later, greenleaf manzanita seedlings numbered 123,500 per acre and after 10 years, 44,450 per acre (McDonald and Fiddler 2001a). Reinvasion of this species was expected, but not to that extent.

A classic example of the consequences of not knowing the past occurred in a clearcut and broadcast-burned compartment on the Challenge Experimental Forest in north-central California. Before harvest and burning, the site consisted of a dense stand of conifers with a deep layer of organic material on the forest floor. Not even a skeleton of a shrub species was present. After burning, seeds of deerbrush germinated by the thousands, and much to the consternation of the forest manager, the area turned "green" almost overnight (McDonald 1983). Subsequent natural generation of desired conifers was highly variable and deficient in places.

As expected in lands having a mediterranean climate with hot, dry summers, wildfire and its frequency is important. A good example concerns pines and shrubs in the southern Cascades (Skinner and Taylor 2006). Older stands that have endured many fires have less shrub seed stored in the soil than young stands that have just emerged from a brushfield or stands that experienced fewer fires. A long interval between burns that promotes dense conifer stands can lead to the absence of such shrubs as bush chinquapin (*Chrysolepis sempervirens* [Kellogg] Hjelmq.) and

Past stand events are a major factor governing which species occur at what locations in the landscape.

huckleberry oak (*Quercus vaccinifolia* Kellogg) that do not develop seed banks in the soil. Another example is the more common phenomenon of California white fir replacing ponderosa pine with continued absence of burning. Here, more shade-enduring shrubs replace those that are prone to burning and, hence, develop better in full sunlight.

On a broader scale, continued absence from burning or logging often leads to a dense forest and a more shady environment that promotes a shift from annual plant species to perennial species after disturbance as in western Oregon (Antos and Halpern 1997) and in the north-central Sierra Nevada (McDonald and Reynolds 1999).

Operational Techniques

When this research program began, vegetation management specialists were doing a little work on manual release and various kinds of mulch materials, but most attention was being given to phenoxy herbicides, especially 2,4-D and 2,4,5-T. These herbicides proved to be biologically worthwhile and cost effective for achieving acceptable survival and growth rates of conifer seedlings. They were so successful that little need was present to have alternative treatments or to learn about their effect on plant communities or plant succession. Consequently, side-by-side vegetation management operational comparisons were rare and information on their effectiveness, cost, and ecological consequences was scarce.

This paper compares most of the vegetation management treatments used for releasing young conifer seedlings in plantations in the Western United States during the study period (McDonald and Fiddler 1989, Walstad and Kuch 1987). These include direct treatments and genetic enhancement, as well as a new concept called "indirect treatments" (McDonald and Fiske 2000). Although this category of treatment is not found in contemporary textbooks as a vegetation management technique, we believe that it is a needed adjunct to the art of vegetation manipulation and worthy of inclusion here.

Direct Treatments

Directly manipulating competing vegetation and reducing its potential to kill or seriously inhibit the growth of young conifer seedlings included the use of herbicides, manual release, mulching, large machines, and grazing animals. We evaluated 21 variations of these treatments and 96 trials in this part of our administrative study (table 7).

Table 7—Kind and number of plantation-release treatments and variations, northern and central California, 1980–2005

Treatment	Variation	Number of trials
Herbicides	3-ft radius	1
	5-ft radius	10
	Whole plot	15
	Cut/spray	4
Manual release	1-, 2-, 3-, 4-, 5-, 6-ft radius, 1 time	20
	2-ft radius, 3 times	1
	5-ft radius, 3 times	1
Mulching	Whole plot, 1 time	4
	Whole plot, 3 times	9
	Whole plot, 5 times	1
	Whole plot, 10 times	3
	1-ft radius	1
	1.5-ft radius	1
	2-ft radius	1
	3-ft radius	1
	4-ft radius	6
	5-ft radius	4
Mechanical	Mechanical only	2
	Mechanical + herbicide	2
Grazing	Cattle	1
	Sheep	2
Genetic enhancement	Nursery run	1
	Wind pollinated	1
	Control pollinated	1
Indirect control	Organic material	2
Control	Shade	1
	To tal	96

Results from the direct treatments are portrayed in a table showing each release technique relative to the control. They were chosen to represent a range of biological responses in each treatment. Data were extracted directly from published tables and figures. Of course, release techniques other than those displayed in the tables were present in each study. For example, the table on herbicides might be from a study that also had two manual release treatments and a control.

Herbicides—

As noted in the three specific studies involving herbicides, at least one chemical in each (fig. 12) gave conifer seedlings a statistically significant growth advantage over counterparts in the control after 10 years (table 8). Sometimes the significant variables were conifer diameter, height, and foliar cover (McDonald and Fiddler 1996, 1999a), or even height, diameter, and crown diameter (McDonald and others 1999a). A general advantage with herbicides is that a single application usually is effective, which tends to lower cost. Exceptions occur, however, with specific shrubs like bearclover (McDonald and others 2004), and situations where large numbers of plants from large seed banks in the soil repeatedly emerge. Here, a second application often is necessary.

> **A general advantage with herbicides is that a single application usually is effective, which tends to lower cost.**

Figure 12—Garlon 3A herbicide is being applied to cut shrubs as a means of vegetation control.

We have noticed that soil-active Velpar persists in the surface soil for about 3 years, which aids conifer seedling growth during the critical early years by almost eliminating competing species. After 3 years, the chemical has moved downward enough to allow shallow-rooted forbs and graminoids to become established. However, deeper rooted shrubs, perennial forbs, and graminoids still cannot establish. By the time the Velpar has moved even deeper in the soil, the conifer seedlings are well established and growing vigorously.

Table 8—Average diameter, foliar cover, and height of conifer seedlings 10 years after treatment in three study areas treated with herbicides, northern and central California

Treatment	Species	Diameter	Foliar cover	Height
		Inches	*Square feet/acre*	*Feet*
Cattle II:				
Velpar	Ponderosa pine	6.59 a	40,900 a	16.51 a
Control		4.58 b	27,850 b	10.94 b
Rocky:				
2,4-D	Douglas-fir	3.55 ab	26,400 ab	18.18 ab
2,4-D + Garlon 4		4.50 a	35,895 a	19.91 ab
Garlon 4		4.05 a	37,750 a	17.94 ab
Cut + Garlon 3A		4.64 a	39,850 a	21.55 a
Control		1.96 b	10,950 c	12.08 b
Latour State Forest:				
Velpar	Ponderosa pine	5.08 a	37,267 a	12.92 a
Garlon		4.12 ab	31,867 b	10.71 b
E scort		3.62 ab	19,200 c	9.89 b
Control		2.80 b	10,133 c	8.23 b

Note: For each study area, treatment means in each column followed by the same letter do not differ statistically at the 0.05 level.

One minor variation related to herbicides was with Aluma-Gel (see footnote 2)—a mixture of aluminum dust and jellied petroleum that generates high heat when burned. Although not an herbicide in the traditional sense, it is considered a chemical, as are herbicides, hence its inclusion here. It was used to treat sprouts from the root crowns of large tanoak stumps. These root crowns constitute regenerative platforms for scores, if not hundreds, of vigorous sprouts, which average over 20 ft tall and 10 ft wide in 10 years (McDonald and Tappeiner 2002). They are so vigorous that they are hard to control, and thus worthy of innovative treatment. On the Plumas National Forest in northern California, shallow trenches that exposed tanoak root crowns were dug around more than 40 stumps, Aluma-Gel was poured in the trenches, and ignited (fig. 13 A, B). The heat, and possibly steam, were supposed to kill the sprout buds (Fiddler and McDonald 1987). Observation several months later showed a large reduction in sprout density, but very few stumps with no sprouts. Hence the treatment was judged unsatisfactory. The reason for lack of success was that the sprout buds were located in protected cracks and crannies on the root burl, and some were deeper than previously thought. These escaped the heat and fire and soon constituted vigorous competition for site resources.

The cost of the traditional herbicide treatment tends to differ with the size of area, method of application, number of applications, and type of chemical. In our studies, the cost ranged from $85 to $137 per acre, not including the chemical.

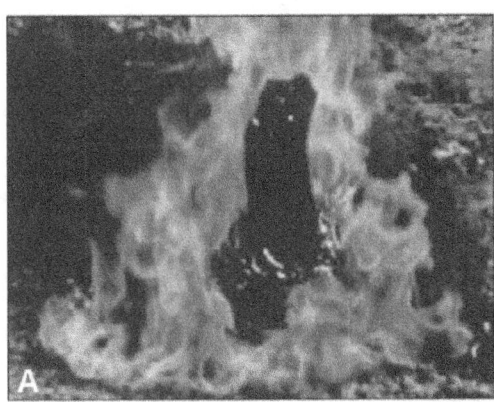 

Figure 13—(A) Flaming Aluma-Gel around a tanoak stump; (B) tanoak sprouts that escaped the heat.

Manual release—

For manual release (fig. 14), a common theme among the three representative study areas was that larger plots, treated most often, yielded a statistical advantage in conifer growth over those in the control (table 9) (McDonald and Fiddler 1995, 1997, data on file[4]). Kind and size of vegetation are important and can affect cost. In two other studies, for example, manually grubbing a 5-ft radius one time around conifer seedlings in a primarily forb and grass community cost $210 per acre, and for chain sawing and shearing vegetation in plots of the same size in a primarily shrub community cost $315 per acre (McDonald and Fiddler 1997, 1999b).

---

[4] Data from unreported study on file with Philip McDonald, Pacific Southwest Research Station, 3644 Avtech Parkway, Redding, CA 96002.

Figure 14—Manual release often is accomplished with hand tools.

Table 9—Average diameter and height of conifer seedlings 10 years after treatment in three study areas treated by manual release (grubbing), northern and central California

Treatment	Species	Diameter	Height
		Inches	*Feet*
Logan:			
4-ft radius, 1 time	Ponderosa pine	3.67 b	8.77 b
4-ft radius, 2 times		4.04 b	9.86 b
4-ft radius, 3 times		4.38 b	10.16 b
Whole plot, 2 times		6.33 a	14.00 a
Control		2.92 b	8.66 b
Harrison Gulch:			
2-ft radius, 1 time	Ponderosa pine	3.04 b	8.45 b
2-ft radius, 3 times		3.32 b	9.19 b
5-ft radius, 1 time		4.18 b	11.52 a
5-ft radius, 3 times		4.68 a	14.27 a
Control		3.12 b	9.64 b
Snag:			
5-ft radius, 1 time	Ponderosa pine	6.61 ab	19.87 ab
5-ft radius, 2 times		6.62 ab	19.89 ab
Whole plot, 1 time		7.18 a	21.80 a
Control		5.68 b	18.53 ab

Note: For each study area, treatment means in each column followed by the same letter do not differ statistically at the 0.05 level.

Duration of growth also is important. In another study in the northern Sierra Nevada, the mixed shrub and herbaceous plant community was manually grubbed each year for the first 3 years after planting, for the first 6 years, and each year for years 4 through 6 (T-second-3). The treated area was a 5-ft radius around 30 to 35 pine seedlings in each of three plots. The total cost for each treatment period was:

Treatment	Time	Cost per acre
	Hours	*Dollars*
T-first-3	27.0	197
T-first-6	65.5	477
T-second-3	82.0	598

It took 60 person-hours to grub the first year of the T-second-3 treatment (McDonald and Fiddler 2007).

The high cost of the T-second-3 treatment was caused not only by the high density of the vegetation but also its development belowground. Some root masses of shrubs had to be split before they could be removed, and others had coalesced for a radius of 2.5 ft or more and had to be grubbed in sections. Still others with deep, rhizomatous root systems, required much work and even then were almost impossible to remove completely. And, based on repeated sampling, several forbs seemed to have an inexhaustible seed supply, whereby grubbing stimulated more plants than were removed. Even the grasses (*Achnatherum* spp.) and brome (*Bromus* spp.) required loosening around the edges before the main clump could be removed.

For the manual release treatment as a whole, costs were quite variable and ranged from $150 to $315 per acre.

Mulching—

Our mulching studies were concerned with widening the application of this method by testing mats that were larger and more durable than those normally used in forestry, and comparing them to the more commonly used smaller, temporary mulches. Results from the three representative study areas for this direct treatment showed that the mulch mats need to be long-lasting, of large size, and in contact with the soil (fig. 15). Soil contact is necessary to transmit water to the soil and prevent it from draining away from the seedling inside the mulch. The large squares of durable polyester and polypropylene created enough competition-free area around the conifer seedlings to promote statistically significant diameter growth and sometimes height growth over counterparts in the control (table 10). More specifically, the larger size of mulch allowed the conifer seedling root system to develop well before the roots of other vegetation could compete with it under the mats. The smaller and short-lived mats did not provide this window of growth (McDonald and Fiddler 1997).

> **Mulch mats need to be long-lasting, of large size, and in contact with the soil.**

Figure 15—A 10- by 10-ft polyester mulch mat on a hillside with all sides tucked in.

Table 10—Average diameter and height of conifer seedlings 5 years after treatment in three study areas treated by mulching (mats), northern and central California

Treatment	Species	Diameter	Height
		Inches	*Feet*
Big Collars:			
4-ft square, sandwich	Ponderosa pine	0.89 b	2.39 b
10-ft square, thin polyester		1.34 a	3.48 a
10-ft square, thick polyester		1.44 a	3.67 a
Control		0.76 b	2.30 b
Harrison Gulch:			
3-ft square, sandwich	Ponderosa pine	1.08 b	3.20 b
Control		1.36 b	4.04 b
Beartrap Ranch:			
10-ft square, polypropylene	Douglas-fir	1.61 a	6.16 b
Control		1.26 b	6.25 b

Note: for each study area, treatment means in each column followed by the same letter do not differ statistically at the 0.05 level.

The total cost of mulching with mats has three components: material, installation, and maintenance. Because mats smaller than 10- by 10-ft square and those made of materials other than polyester and polypropylene proved to be ineffective in a wide variety of plant communities, we present cost information only for the larger, durable ones. Installation generally is routine, except on steep slopes. In one study on a slope of 30 percent and initially bare soil (Big Collars), the upper edge of the mats had to be placed in a shallow trench and backfilled to keep them from sliding downhill in the winter. This of course, increased the cost. Maintenance typically involves visiting each mat at least once each year and tying down windblown corners with pins or stakes. The total cost over a 5-year period, was $1,984 per acre (McDonald and others 1994b).

At Beartrap Ranch, the plant community was composed of forbs, ferns, and graminoids on a slope of 50 percent. Because of strong incessant winds, each 10- by 10-ft square mulch of light-weight polypropylene was placed over the existing vegetation and held down by thirteen 9-in metal pins. The combination of expensive material, steep slope, and strong wind increased the total cost, especially the installation and maintenance costs. Altogether, the total cost was $2,059 per acre (McDonald and others 1994a).

In another study (Mulches), we wished to extend the mulching technique to control sprouting shrubs—a plant community rarely tested with mats. Here the mats were 10-ft squares of heavy polyester felt applied around planted Douglas-fir seedlings and over burned stubs of shrub tanoak (*Lithocarpus densiflorus* [Hook. & Arn.] Rehder var. *echinoides* [R.Br. Campst.] Abrams). Hence the mulches never touched the ground. The slope was 40 percent, the aspect northeast, and the soil deep. In spite of the large treated area, growth of the Douglas-fir seedlings was almost nil and mortality was higher than expected. Further investigation showed a miniature desert beneath the mulches. Apparently, water traveled through the mulches internally, wicked off in the air at the lower end, and never reached the soil near the seedlings. Shrub tanoak is a vigorous sprouter after disturbance and it soon created mounds of sprouts under the mats. These tended to overheat, and after 4 years, almost all of the sprouts were dead. However, the mounds necessitated additional maintenance because they tended to pull up the hold-down pins on the mat edges. Over a 4-year period, the cost was more than $2,600 per acre (McDonald and others 1989).

Mechanical release—

In the two mechanical release studies in our research program (Fiddler and McDonald 1997, Fiddler and others 2000), cutting 12- and 16-year-old shrubs with large machines (fig. 16) did not statistically enhance diameter and height growth of pine seedlings over counterparts in the control at the 0.05 level (table 11). Rapid resprouting of the vigorous shrubs was the reason. The cost was $225 and $218 per acre, respectively.

Figure 16—A Trac Mac at work in an older plantation. Note the layer of shredded vegetation in the foreground.

Table 11—Average diameter and height of conifer seedlings 10 years after treatment in two study areas treated by mechanical release (machines), northern and central California

Treatment	Species	Diameter	Height
		Inches	*Feet*
Third Water:			
Trac Mac	Ponderosa and Jeffrey pine	4.76 b	15.08 b
Control		4.40 b	14.95 b
Big Tunnel:			
Hydro-Ax	Ponderosa pine	7.56 b	18.99 b
Control		6.49 b	16.68 b

Note: For each stud area, treatment means in each column followed by the same letter do not differ statistically at the 0.05 level.

Because the primary competition to the conifer seedlings in both studies was from well-developed sprouting shrubs, an additional treatment was called for. This was 2,4-D, applied when the resprouting shrubs were 1 and 2 years old. With combined mechanical and chemical treatment, crown cover of ponderosa and Jeffrey pine saplings at Third Water was significantly increased over counterparts in the control after 11 growing seasons. At Big Tunnel, average ponderosa pine diameter, crown cover, and height were statistically increased over pines in the control after 11 years. The herbicide added $49.00 at Third Water and $48.00 at Big Tunnel for total costs of $273 and $266 per acre. The role of the grasses relative to treatment is interesting. At Third Water, the number of grass plants was described as few and the size as small during the entire study. At Big Tunnel the density of the grass (mostly *Achnatherum* spp.) in the three treatments was mechanical, 0 plants per acre; mechanical and chemical, 1,246,667 per acre; and control, 44,000 plants per acre at the end of the study. Diary records noted "grass in these treatments is virtually the only grass in the entire plantation."

Grazing animals—
Much evidence shows that to be effective, release must take place when the conifer seedlings are young and the competing vegetation also is young and not yet capturing many site resources. Grazing cattle (fig. 17) in young plantations often is regarded as being too risky—the conifer seedlings are trampled, have their tops nipped, or are pulled from the ground. In this study, cattle grazed the plantation only 3 months after planting with no damage to the seedlings (McDonald and Fiddler 1999a). In spite of this good start, grazing by cattle never significantly enhanced the growth of the ponderosa pine seedlings over the 10-year study (table 12).

Grazing by cattle never significantly enhanced the growth of the ponderosa pine seedlings over the 10-year study.

Figure 17—The cow in the center of this figure is one of many utilizing the vegetation in this ponderosa pine plantation.

Table 12—Average diameter, foliar cover, and height of conifer seedlings 10 years after treatment in three study areas treated by grazing animals, northern and central California

Treatment	Species	Diameter	Foliar cover	Height
		Inches	*Square feet/acre*	*Feet*
Cattle II:				
Grazing	Ponderosa pine	5.18 b	29,800 b	12.39 b
Control		4.58 b	27,850 b	10.94 b
Sheep I:				
Grazing	Ponderosa pine	4.20 b	26,572 b	10.80 b
Control		3.90 b	15,246 b	10.20 b
Sheep II:				
Grazing	Jeffrey pine	1.90 b	8,276 b	4.70 b
Control		2.20 b	10,890 b	5.20 b

Note: For each study area, treatment means in each column followed by the same letter do not differ statistically at the 0.05 level.

Sheep often are the animals of choice for wildland grazing (fig. 18). They are well suited to the dry, rough, and often shrub-inhabited terrain typical of conifer plantations in the Western United States. But as for cattle, skepticism remains that the risk of damage to the conifer seedlings outweighs the gains from utilizing the forage, particularly when the seedlings are young. Sharrow (1994) noted: "Forest

Figure 18—This large band of sheep eats a lot of forage, but not enough to significantly reduce competition to the conifer seedlings.

managers acceptance of sheep as a biological tool is currently limited by lack of site-specific data detailing the ecological and economic costs and benefits associated with prescription sheep grazing in forests."

In both of the sheep studies (McDonald and Fiddler 1993a, McDonald and others 1996), at least 30 species of plants were present, and forage in the form of shrubs, forbs, and grasses was plentiful. Apparently this forage was preferred, and little damage was done to conifer seedlings at any time, even when they were young and contained new, succulent foliage. After 10 years, grazing by sheep did not significantly increase average diameter, foliar cover, or height of pine seedlings (table 12).

For an at-a-glance evaluation, the five major direct vegetation manipulation treatments are summarized in terms of cost (table 13) and application, limitations, and effectiveness (table 14).

> After 10 years, grazing by sheep did not significantly increase average diameter, foliar cover, or height of pine seedlings.oe

Table 13—Relative cost of the five direct vegetation management treatments

Treatment	Cost
	Dollars per acre[a]
Herbicides	85–137
Manual release	150–315
Mulching	1,984–2,600
Mechanical	218–225
Grazing animals	0[b]

[a] U.S. Department of Labor wage rate of June 1993.
[b] Income from grazing is assumed to equal the cost of administering the allotment.

Table 14—Summary of direct treatments and variations: application, limitations, and effectiveness

Treatment and variation	Application	Limitations	Effectiveness
Herbicides:			
2,4-D	Broad	Social pressure, grasses	Effective
Garlon 3A	Broad	Social pressure, grasses	Effective
Garlon 4	Broad	Social pressure, grasses	Effective
Roundup	Broad	Social pressure, grasses	Effective
Velpar	Broad	Social pressure	Effective
Manual release:			
1- to 4-ft radius	Narrow	Shrubs, hardwoods	Ineffective
5-ft radius	Broad	Cost	Effective
Whole plot	Broad	Cost	Effective
Mulching:			
Materials other than polyester and polypropylene	Narrow	Decay, cost	Ineffective
Sizes smaller than 5-ft radius	Narrow	Treatment size	Ineffective
Polyester and polypropylene	Broad	Cost, shrubs	Moderate
Mechanical:			
Trac Mac and Hydro-Ax	Broad	Vegetation other than large shrubs, terrain	Ineffective without herbicide followup
Grazing animals:			
Cattle and sheep	Narrow	Multiple years, timing of grazing, type of vegetation, utilization of forage	Ineffective

Genetic Enhancement

When we began this study, a key question was paramount in our minds: Would genetically-enhanced ponderosa pine seedlings outgrow nursery-run seedlings **at an early age**? This was critical. If they would not exhibit rapid juvenile growth, then their worth as a vegetation management tool would be limited. Shortly after outplanting from the nursery bed in 1989, control-pollinated pine seedlings were statistically taller (fig. 19) and had larger diameters just below the cotyledon scar than wind-pollinated and nursery-run counterparts at the 5 percent level (McDonald and others 1994c):

Would genetically-enhanced ponderosa pine seedlings outgrow nursery-run seedlings at an early age?

Treatment	Height (ft)	Diameter (in)
Nursery-run	0.48a	0.16a
Wind-pollinated	0.49a	0.17a
Control-pollinated	0.57b	0.19b
Standard error	0.01	0.01

Values in each column followed by the same letter do not differ statistically at the 0.05 level.

Figure 19—The rows of control-pollinated seedlings are significantly taller than wind-pollinated and nursery-run seedlings in this nursery bed.

By fall 1991, or after three growing seasons in the field, only the height of control-pollinated seedlings differed statistically from nursery-run seedlings with competition, which was a vigorous stand of shrubs, hardwood sprouts, forbs, and grasses. For free-to-grow seedlings, mean height continued to differ statistically among the three genetic classes, but only control-pollinated seedling diameter differed significantly from that of nursery-run seedlings. Subsequent analysis of growth during the third through sixth growing seasons (1992 to 1995), indicated that we had lost the statistical differences for pine height and diameter among genetic classes when growing with competition. For seedlings without competition, control-pollinated seedlings continued to be statistically taller than nursery-run seedlings (fig. 20); mean values were 9.7 versus 8.4 ft, respectively. All other statistical differences had disappeared (McDonald and others 1999b). Plainly, early release was needed just as much for genetically improved ponderosa pine seedlings as for nursery-run seedlings.

Early release was needed just as much for genetically improved ponderosa pine seedlings as for nursery-run seedlings.

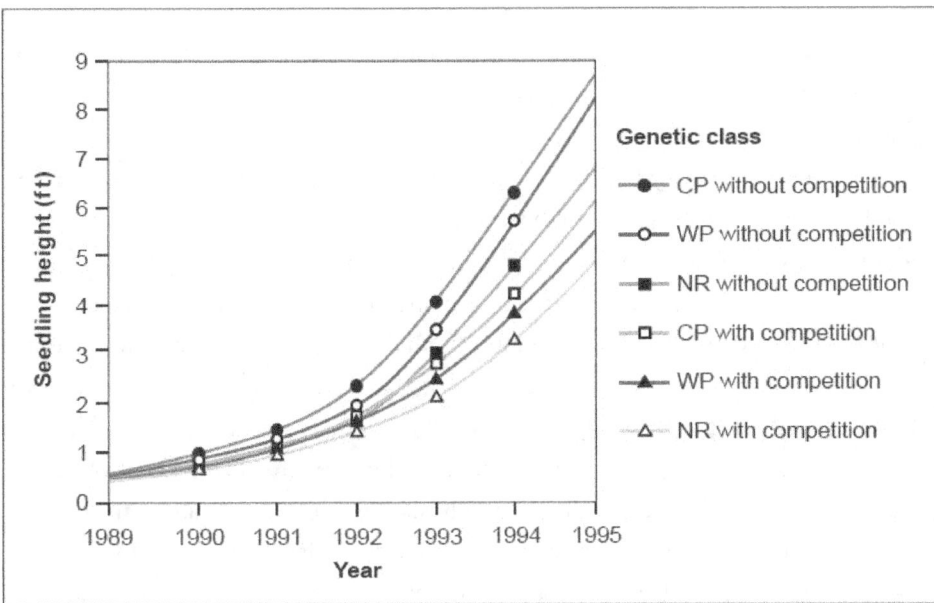

Figure 20—Of all the comparisons, only the control-pollinated (CP) seedlings without competition differed from nursery-run (NR) counterparts. WP = wind pollinated.

Indirect Treatments

Most forest vegetation managers know that organic matter often contains legions of damping-off fungi and other organisms that inhibit the development of tiny radicals (roots). They also know that shade inhibits the growth of many, if not most, competing species as well as that of conifer seedlings. Unfortunately, little data have been collected on vegetation in these environments and results are mostly anecdotal.

In one of our northern California studies (Lee's Summit), the area was broadcast burned in the spring when the slash and logging debris were dry and the soil was wet. This resulted in removal of most of the aboveground material and created areas where the soil was disturbed by harvest and other areas where it was covered with at least a 1-in layer of organic material. Two years after the burn, when the organic matter had decomposed, we quantified the density of various species and categories of species in both the mineral soil and organic matter areas (table 15).

Table 15—Plant density 2 years after site preparation at two levels of organic matter (as a percentage of ground cover), northern California

| Organic matter | Density | | | |
	Deerbrush	Manzanita Gr	asses	Forbs
Percentage	- - - - - - - - - - Number of plants/acre - - - - - - - - - -			
70–90	1,917	250	417	1,333
10–20	3,750	2,250	14,250	1,250

We found that the area, which once was covered with organic matter, had less than one-seventh the amount of deerbrush, greenleaf manzanita, and grass seedlings than the area that was mostly bare mineral soil.

On the Hoopa Valley Reservation in northern California, the Native Americans who live there value the tanoak tree for many reasons, including its acorns as a favorite source of food. Typical stands tend to be too dense with trees that have narrow crowns and produce few acorns. An ongoing goal is to lightly thin such stands to widen crowns and provide more sunlight to them. The root-crown sprouts that develop from the cut stumps are not wanted and steps must be taken to remove them or greatly reduce their vigor.

Our replicated study involved 120 stumps with three treatments: control, charring the sprouts with a weed burner for 4 consecutive years, and cutting the bole twice (double decapitation). The theory of double decapitation is that cytokinins and giberellins accumulate at the cut surface of the stump where they prevent auxins from inhibiting the lateral buds. Removal of the upper stump after hormone translocation occurs may reduce the amount of hormones available to stimulate the growth of dormant buds. Two years after the last burning, the number of sprouts per stump was significantly larger with burning than with double decapitation or the control (Wilkinson and others 1997). Mean height of sprouts after burning was significantly lower with burning than in the other two treatments as well. The mobilization of growth hormones to the top of the cut stump apparently did not occur in tanoak, rendering double decapitation no different than the control.

Other unexpected factors influenced sprout height and number. In the double decapitation treatment and control, sprouts were infected with mold. Most sprout tips eventually died from the infection and a general decrease in vigor of entire sprouts was evident. New sprouts from the base of burned sprouts were noticeably more tender and of a brighter green color than sprouts in the other two treatments. These were heavily browsed by deer and noticeably shortened by them. Thus mold and deer browsing became part of the treatments.

Another example of a shade-mediated environment is that created by group-selection cutting. This method, which is part of an uneven-age silvicultural system, involves the removal of groups of trees to create small openings up to about 2 acres. Several of these openings, scattered throughout a stand, usually are harvested together on a cyclic basis. The cycle often is 10 or 15 years. There is no rotation, and cutting continues in perpetuity, usually removing clusters of mature trees. The group-selection method often is perceived as being "gentle" on the land, its vegetation, and its creatures, and hence is applied where the landowner desires to harvest some trees periodically, but where logging damage is slight and most ecosystem processes are not disrupted. Findings are reported from two studies on group-selection cutting.

In a 1964 study on the Challenge Experimental Forest, 48 openings, 30, 60, and 90 ft in diameter, were created on a high-quality site (McDonald and Abbott 1994). Smaller logging slash was spread out on opening edges with a bulldozer, and larger concentrations were burned in adjacent skid roads. After 10 years, more than 9,800 conifer and 1,445 hardwood seedlings per acre, at least 4 years old, accumulated in each opening (fig. 21). In general, tree seedlings and shrubs were tallest in the center of the largest openings and shortest in the smaller opening and near opening edges. Overall, shrubs had narrow crowns with only one or two stems per clump,

Figure 21—Ten-year-old conifer regeneration in a group-selection opening on the Challenge Experimental Forest. Each swizzle stick denotes a seedling.

tall stems, and a generally weak appearance. Many had died. The density of green-leaf manzanita, for example, was 509 per acre, foliar cover was less than 1 percent, and average dominant height was 2.6 ft. In a nearby clearcutting on a similar site, greenleaf manzanita averaged 16 times more density, 18 times more foliar cover with five to eight stems per clump, and was twice as tall.

After 28 years, the openings remain well stocked with conifer saplings, hardwoods, and herbaceous species. Dominance was expressed by the more shade-tolerant conifers, especially California white fir (fig. 22) and tanoak. Although many shrubs, forbs, and graminoids were present, their foliar cover and height were far less than that of the dominant saplings.

Figure 22—Twenty eight-year-old conifer saplings in a group-selection opening on the Challenge Experimental Forest.

The study on group-selection cutting on the Boggs Mountain State Forest began in 1988 and took place in nine openings that ranged from 0.2 to 1.6 acres. After 4 years, the vegetation was characterized by many species, a huge number of plants, and limited foliar cover and height (McDonald and others 1997). However, average dominant height of all categories of vegetation (ponderosa pines, shrubs, manzanita, ferns, graminoids, and forbs) was greater near plot centers.

We were particularly interested in the effect of opening size and distance from edge on the growth of naturally seeded and planted ponderosa pines (McDonald and others 2009). At Boggs Mountain, the difference between the two regeneration types for both stem diameter and height was dramatic. After nine growing seasons, the average height and diameter of planted seedlings was 2.4 and 2.7 times that of natural seedlings, respectively. If the seedlings were naturally seeded, growth seemed to plod along regardless of opening size and distance from edge. But for planted seedlings, distance from edge had a much stronger effect, particularly in larger openings.

Discussion

In the material that follows, results from the plant community, biological influences, and operational techniques are discussed with emphasis on each and how the basic tenets in each interact with the others.

Plant Community Development

A major need in forest ecology and vegetation management today is knowledge on the plant community that develops after different levels of natural and human-caused disturbance. Sometimes people frown on human disturbance, but overall disturbance is necessary and beneficial as Atzet and Martin (1992) noted: "Disturbance brings change that helps maintain compositional, structural, and functional diversity, helps to select adapted, resilient individuals, and helps to dampen the effects of minor environmental oscillations and extremes. Change is an essential ingredient of healthy ecosystems." Furthermore, Reice (1994) suggested that disturbance is ubiquitous and frequent relative to the lifespans of the dominant taxa. Thus communities are always recovering from the last disturbance. And, the size and extent of the disturbed areas modifies the ensuing disturbances, creating an ever-changing environment.

Consequently, vegetation managers need to develop knowledge on changes in the plant community over time. The density and growth of individual species and their eventual ascendance or decline, is particularly important. Equally important are the changes to plant communities brought about by different levels of human-caused disturbance. Such levels, termed treatments, often alter the amount of competition to planted conifer seedlings, but seldom have a long-term effect on the species composition of the community, at least for the first 10 years.

Unfortunately, knowledge on plant species composition and development after disturbance generally is lacking and often tied to a few competitive species that limit the survival and growth of economic species. Such is the case for many species in almost all major categories of vegetation, some of which are notorious for their limiting effect on conifer seedling survival and growth in young plantations.

After nine growing seasons, the average height and diameter of planted seedlings was 2.4 and 2.7 times that of natural seedlings.

A major need in forest ecology and vegetation management today is knowledge on the plant community that develops after different levels of natural and human-caused disturbance.

Consequently, vegetation managers need to develop knowledge on changes in the plant community over time.

In the 5-year study on the Challenge Experimental Forest (McDonald 1999), the vast majority of species became established early and persisted throughout the study period. Several species were present for only a few years and then disappeared, but all categories of vegetation were represented in this decline. Other species invaded later in the study, but almost all of these were annual and perennial forbs, as well as graminoids. Density of all plant species increased more than 4 times during the study, and foliar cover more than 18 times. After five growing seasons, enough plants were present to cast a solid shadow over about 40 percent of the land surface. Thus, space was available for additional horizontal development, but although increasing, the rate of increase slowed each year through the second to fifth growing seasons. Increasing competition for soil moisture, nutrients, and sunlight, and occupancy of the most favorable microsites are probable reasons.

Of interest, was that 31 percent of the species present during the study never had more than 0.5 ft^2 of cover. Conversely, after the first year, less than 25 percent of the species present contributed over 90 percent of foliar cover. Severe browsing of some shrubs by deer early in the study may have aided their development and dominance potential. Deerbrush and whiteleaf manzanita (*Arctostaphylos viscida* C. Parry) for example, seemed to have benefited by damage to the main stem. This led to the development of multiple stems at an early age, and increased their potential for higher foliar cover.

We began the analysis of plant species diversity in 21 study areas (McDonald and Fiddler 2006) with the idea that, because most plantations were located in the general forest zone on land capable of producing an economic crop, a certain amount of similarity in species would be present. We tried to relate the number of species at the beginning of studies and after 10 years, to six categories of vegetation, to site productivity, to different ages of vegetation, and to possible core species with limited success. Plainly, species diversity in young conifer plantations in northern and central California is highly variable and related to the interactions of more variables than those we evaluated.

However, knowledge from this study should be helpful in a larger sense. Sometimes opponents of intensive forest management blame the loss of plant species on site preparation and release. Vegetation managers often have trouble countering this argument. Now managers have some information, at least for environments similar to those in this study. They can count on a broad range of plant species, an average of about 25 species in six categories, and some core species and genera. Together, these species and the planted conifer seedlings protect the site, are useful to wildlife, and promote ecological diversity. They provide opportunity for future

Plainly, species diversity in young conifer plantations in northern and central California is highly variable and related to the interactions of more variables than those we evaluated.

manipulation not only toward a broad array of desired values and commodities, but also toward the forest that was present originally.

The comparison of vegetation development after 10 years in the three differing communities manipulated by several release treatments provides two important points: (1) an increasing shrub density often causes fewer species in the plantation and a broader range in foliar cover and height than in other communities, even if the range in number of plants per acre is lower; and (2) whatever the plant community, a large range in number of species per acre is present and their range in density is large (table 3). The cubic-volume values (foliar cover × height) also could be useful to wildlife biologists and fire ecologists because they provide an estimate of the amount of browse and fuel.

Whatever the plant community, a large range in number of species per acre is present and their range in density is large.

Biological Influences

We never fail to be amazed at how well some plant species in the California landscape are adapted. Plants in such genera as *Arctostaphylos*, *Ceanothus*, *Chamaebatia*, *Chrysolepis*, *Pteridium*, and *Quercus*, which arise from both above- and belowground propagules, are noteworthy. We have observed that mature plants from these genera are rarely killed by insects and disease and even more rarely by drought, heat, frost, and other abiotic agents. Several stems in a patch or clump may die, but the plant lives on.

The internal moisture stress data help to substantiate how well some plant species adapt to the most limiting environmental factor in most of California—soil moisture. The predawn minimum moisture stress values for 5-year-old ponderosa pine seedlings were very low in all treatments, which indicated that the roots were efficient at gathering moisture from the soil even at the end of a typical long, hot summer. Predawn stress values also were very low for tanoak and snowbrush. This is not surprising, as plants of these species, which were 3 years old at the time of sampling, probably were sprouts from root crowns that had access to parent-plant root systems. The predawn minimum moisture values for deerbrush and greenleaf manzanita, particularly in the least effective treatments where competition was fierce, were a classic example of adaptation. Plainly, their roots were unable to recharge their systems with water overnight, yet they were able to withstand severe internal moisture stress without wilting or dying. Indeed, deerbrush endured high stress for the entire day without ill effects.

Maximum internal moisture stress in all the plant species that we tested ranged from 18 to more than 42 atmospheres in the least effective treatments with no observable wilting. As a whole, these species in these treatments had higher predawn values, earlier peaking, higher maximum values, and the need to endure long periods of high stress. Capability to limit respiration at high temperatures, ability to intake at least a little soil moisture early in the morning, to be able to photosynthesize at relatively high internal moisture stress levels, and to limit transpiration, are all valuable adaptations that limited damage to leaves and stems.

We also have found that plants in the early seral community of young conifer plantations in California follow most, if not all, of the five classical regeneration strategies of Grime (1979) and one or more of the three traditional successional pathways of Connell and Slatyer (1977). Rarely is the vegetation in a plantation dominated by a single class of plants or by plants from a single regeneration strategy (McDonald and Radosevich 1992). Consequently, most competitive plant species present after site preparation originate from a variety of structures and employ different strategies that impart unique advantages to members. These are "instant" site occupancy by burgeoning sprouts and seedlings from thousands of dormant, but viable, seeds in the soil, saturation of an area by shade-tolerant seedlings and windblown seeds, or rapid underground growth by rhizomes. Where a number of species having different regeneration strategies are present, dominance accrues to those species that become largest first. All three successional pathways seem to be active in new plantations, and together with the regeneration strategies, indicate that a large variety of well-adapted species are present, each with unique ability.

The dominant species of the near future will be those whose regeneration strategies result in early dominance.

Based on many of our operational studies as well as the study on the Challenge Experimental Forest, the mode or process of plant succession is best characterized as "modified" environmental succession. The dominant species of the near future will be those whose regeneration strategies result in early dominance. Sprouting shrubs and hardwoods with rapidly increasing foliar cover and height are good examples. As the crowns of trees and shrubs close, and the high density of the annuals and graminoids decreases, more shade-tolerant conifers and perennials will become established. Thus succession will occur through environmental modification. It is not classical replacement of one stage of species by another stage, however, because the first stage will be present for many years. Species of random origin, especially those from windblown seeds, will not be a major part of the understory plant community. Plants from the seed bank in the soil will not be a major part of this community either. However they will have accomplished their mission because the storehouse in the soil will have been replenished.

Longer term, the number of plant species in the plantation likely will decline. A good example took place in a mature brushfield on a harsh site near Mount Shasta. Before site preparation and planting in 1962, three tall, vigorous shrub species dominated in the area. After 5 years, the plant community consisted of 6 shrubs,

10 forbs, and 1 grass (McDonald and Abbott 1997). When the study ended in 1992 (after 31 years) the community consisted of five shrubs, two forbs, and one grass. However, two shrubs, both forbs, and the grass consisted of only a few plants in the entire study area. The progression from 3 to 17 and then back to 3 species may be anathema to some people. But this gap in species richness probably is only an interim phenomenon. The traditional arborescent pioneer species, ponderosa pine, is now established on plots with the least amount of competition and 30 years later is growing at the potential of the site. This is the first step in plant succession. Eventually shade-tolerant conifers also will become established (or planted) and form the mixed-conifer forest that originally occupied the area. It is likely that more species of plants will find this forest environment conducive to establishment than if the area had remained a brushfield (McDonald and Fiddler 2001b), and plant species richness likely will increase again.

Operational Techniques

Over the years, an amazing number of direct control techniques have been attempted to control competing vegetation in young conifer plantations in California: dynamite, plastic buckets over spouting stumps, newspaper mulches, copper nails, bleach, sheets of plywood, rotary mowers, and blow torches to name a few. One early study in California involved a sample of 2,254 stumps of sprouting oaks and large shrubs (Bruce 1936). Treated vegetation was live oak (*Quercus* spp.), black oak (*Quercus* spp.), toyon (*Heteromeles* sp.), mountain mahogany (*Cercocarpus* spp.), prunus (*Prunus* spp.), coffee berry (*Rhamnus* spp.), fremontia (*Fremontodendron* spp.) and sprouting manzanita (*Arctostaphylos* spp.). "The work consisted of treating sprouting stumps with various chemicals, under various conditions of concentration, location, season, and mode of preparation of the stump." Treatments included sodium chloride, carbon bisulfide, arsenite, cupric sulfate, ferrous sulphate, stove oil, diesel oil, sulfuric acid, calcium oxychloride, pyradine, and ammonium thiocyanate. Some chemicals were applied to sprouting stumps, desprouted stumps, and even excavated roots of desprouted stumps. Several mixes of chemicals, kinds of application, and timing were effective at killing sprouts or preventing sprouting. However, the use of most, if not all of these products, would be questionable today.

Herbicides were suspended by the USDA Forest Service in March 1984 in response to federal court rulings (Click and others 1989). This moratorium was lifted in January 1991, but during the 7-year interval, the variety of treatments used by vegetation managers increased even more. Some of these treatments included the

Over the years, an amazing number of direct control techniques have been attempted to control competing vegetation in young conifer plantations in California: dynamite, plastic buckets over spouting stumps, newspaper mulches, copper nails, bleach, sheets of plywood, rotary mowers, and blow torches to name a few.

use of concentrated fire around stumps using Aluma-Gel, trenching and planting on berms, and a host of mulch materials. Most of these were performed "to buy time" until the moratorium was lifted or better techniques became available.

Herbicides—

Many factors influence the ability of an herbicide to control undesirable vegetation. These include the ability of the chemical to penetrate the leaves, the availability of enough water in the leaves and stems to translocate the herbicide to the intended plant part, and the capability of the herbicide to effectively damage the plant to the point that it becomes moribund. More than in any other treatment, herbicides tend to kill the plant, not just its top. Several morphological and physiological factors are important and relate to leaf age and plant size. Young leaves have not had time to develop thick epidermal layers or oily and waxy coverings and therefore are more easily penetrated by the chemical. It stands to reason that small plants are more easily affected than large plants because they have less biomass and less sprouting potential. Small plants also are developing at a time when internal moisture levels and photosynthesis are high, and thus translocation and assimilation of the herbicide are increased. It follows that as summer progresses, stomates in the leaves open less fully or for shorter intervals, internal moisture stress increases, photosynthesis declines, and herbicide intake is much reduced. For these reasons, our studies with herbicides took place in young plantations less than 4 years old when the vegetation, whether from seeds or sprouts, was of sufficient size and development to treat effectively.

The three representative studies denoted in table 8 also took place in a wide variety of plant communities that ranged from mostly tough, aggressive shrubs to those containing a mixture of shrubs, forbs, ferns, and grasses. One study also included sprouts from hardwood trees. The studies also were located on site qualities that ranged from medium to above average. Thus the results indicate that herbicides are effective on a wide range of plant communities on most sites at a reasonable cost.

> **The results indicate that herbicides are effective on a wide range of plant communities on most sites at a reasonable cost.**

Manual release—

Of the five classical direct-control vegetation management techniques, manual release is probably the easiest to implement. It requires only a hand tool; however, the work is hard, dirty, and potentially dangerous. Manual release in California was first done in the 1970s by local people with negotiated contracts for relatively small areas. This soon changed to competitive bids that were awarded to the lowest bidder. Often, local contractors would hire local people and owing to inexperience, would default on their contracts. Soon a performance bond was required, which hastened conversion to experienced contractors with established crews, many from outside the area. Consequently, the practice of manual release evolved from a few individuals to groups of people working on larger units for more money (Fiddler and McDonald 1990). Over the years, a wide variety of people have organized to bid on manual release contracts, including environmentalists, townspeople, loggers, students, churchgoers, and Russians. By far the largest group, however, was Latinos.

The three representative studies shown in table 9 took place in plant communities that were composed primarily of shrubs; forbs, ferns, and grasses; and a mixture of woody and herbaceous vegetation. The shrubs, although rated as aggressive, were treated when they were young and small. The three representative studies and others indicate that manual release is most effective if the vegetation is treated when young and when the plant community is mostly forbs and grasses. But even then, a second release treatment is almost always necessary.

Mulches—

We tried to broaden the application of this method by studying many kinds and sizes of mulch mats in several plant communities. We also fully quantified costs by including maintenance for several years. We learned that mats do have a place in the vegetation manager's handbook provided they are large, durable, and in contact with the ground. Mats can even be used effectively in a sprouting shrub community. However, the large, durable mats tend to be costly, and a lack of decomposition in the center could eventually strangle the seedling. Mats work best if they simply disintegrate in place, or become covered with soil and other organic debris. But if they flop around or pieces of them become scattered, then they are aesthetically displeasing to people passing by. Gathering them would be yet another cost. The total cost could be mitigated if manufacturers would standardize mulches to a given material, size, color, and time to degrade. They might even produce camouflaged mulch that would blend into the natural environment in visually sensitive areas.

A possible advantage to using mulch mats is the amount and longevity of moisture held under them. At Beartrap Ranch, for instance, mulches were applied over the existing grass and forb community. Heat from the mulches quickly killed these plants and formed another mulch, in effect becoming an organic mulch under a mulch (McDonald and others 1994a). This organic material absorbed moisture and the soil under it stayed moist well into the growing season. It also temporarily blocked at least some upward-moving soil moisture from escaping through the pores of the mats. Applying mats early in the spring when the soil is at field

Manual release is most effective if the vegetation is treated when young and when the plant community is mostly forbs and grasses.

Mats do have a place in the vegetation manager's handbook provided they are large, durable, and in contact with the ground.

capacity is suggested because it would lock in soil moisture under them. This, of course, applies to mats in general, whether installed over existing vegetation or bare ground.

Mechanical release—

For monetary, political, or accessibility reasons, plantation release often cannot be done in time, and the returning vegetation, often of sprouting shrubs, grows wide and tall. Consequently, untreated plantations that are 10 years or older are present in the West. Conifers in many of these plantations are penalized by heavy competition and a trend of decreasing annual height increments. Controlling vegetation of this size and level of development often is both difficult and expensive with commonly applied methods such as manual release or grazing. Most herbicides do not work well on tall shrubs and hardwoods either. Another factor to consider is the conifer seedlings. They are approaching sapling or small-pole size and, although taller than the shrubs, have thin bark that causes broadcast burning to be impractical as well. Being taller than the shrubs is no guarantee that the conifer seedlings will grow at the potential of the site (McDonald and Abbott 1997).

Results from our two studies on mechanical release reinforce the need for an herbicide application soon after treatment with the large machines. Not to do so renders the work of the machines ineffective.

The surge of grasses in the combined mechanical and herbicide treatment at Big Tunnel follows the trend noted earlier in the biological control and exclusion section. It also is similar to findings for the most effective herbicide treatments in some of our other studies (McDonald and Everest 1996, McDonald and Fiddler 1999c, McDonald and others 1996). Cheat grass (*Bromus tectorum* L.) and other annual grasses were common in these studies and tended to increase in density 3 to 5 years after the conifer seedlings were planted. Becoming established well after the conifers were planted, being shorter than the conifers, and having roots that did not grow as deep as the conifers, meant that the grasses were less competitive than most invading shrubs and hardwoods.

Grazing animals—

Managers often think of plantations as being all cost and no income for many years, or at least until commercial thinning. But some plantations can provide immediate income in terms of nonwood values. Plantations may provide a pleasant view to the passing motorist, and provide sustenance to several species of wildlife as well as cattle and sheep. For grazing animals, the key is that at least some species in the plant community be palatable. As noted earlier, most plant communities in northern and central California plantations have many categories of vegetation and contain

The need is for an herbicide application soon after treatment with large machines. Not to do so renders the work of the machines ineffective.

many species, several of which are palatable. If the grazing animals concentrate on this vegetation, it could mean less damage to conifer seedlings.

Because the study on cattle and both studies on sheep did not demonstrate a significant gain in pine seedling growth, the use of grazing animals as a release tool for the vegetation manager is questionable. Current practices, at least as practiced in northern California, have several weaknesses. To begin with, the animals are seldom used the first season after logging or burning—the perception is that not enough forage is present and that damage to the conifer seedlings would be severe. In addition, when used in subsequent growing seasons, the timing is poor. Traditionally, the cattle and sheep feed at lower elevations until the forage is gone, then they are trucked to higher elevations in the forest zone. Usually, this is too late. Most of the early, tender, and more nutritious growth has become hard and mature, or eaten by other herbivores. And even when the animals are present for wildland grazing, the tendency is to herd them to the most nutritious forage, and remove them before secondary species and plant parts are all that remain. The end result is that grazing is too little, too late, and utilization is never high enough to weaken the competing vegetation to the point that the conifer seedlings have a significant growth advantage over counterparts in the control.

Several steps can be taken to enhance grazing as a viable vegetation management tool. Truck the animals to the selected area the first growing season after planting and as soon as possible in the spring to utilize the vegetation while it is tender and nutritious. Once there, the animals should be held to graze as much vegetation as possible even if it means consuming less than prime forage. If these conditions cannot be met, the range deteriorates, or damage to the conifer seedlings becomes intolerable, then this method will not be viable from the standpoint of seedling survival and growth. In our studies the pines did not benefit, but the cattle and sheep did, and the owners were pleased with the low cost and good weight gains of their animals. In a broader sense, the return from the land of wool, meat, and lambs not only helps the landowner, but also the world, which is ever in need of more food and fiber.

Availability, cost, ease of application, effectiveness, and speedy results are factors that can be used to evaluate each direct treatment. When they are packaged and compared as a whole, the composite with the highest rating is herbicides.

Genetic enhancement—

At this point, we need to mention that genetic enhancement of conifer **trees** constitutes a broad program for improving conifer tree growth, stem form, and resistance to insects and diseases. Our study was concerned with a very narrow part of

Because the study on cattle and both studies on sheep did not demonstrate a significant gain in pine seedling growth, the use of grazing animals as a release tool for the vegetation manager is questionable.

Availability, cost, ease of application, effectiveness, and speedy results are factors that can be used to evaluate each direct treatment. When they are packaged and compared as a whole, the composite with the highest rating is herbicides.

genetic enhancement. The early finding that genetically enhanced ponderosa pine **seedlings** growing with competition significantly outgrew nursery-run seedlings seemed to open a promising and meaningful door in vegetation management. However, enhanced seedlings grew no better than the nursery-run seedlings after a few years.

This leads to the larger question: "Do genetically improved seedlings have a place in forest vegetation management?" In this study, and in a much larger trial, the outcome is clouded, but as noted later, more research is needed. The larger trial was with slash pine (*Pinus elliottii* Engelm.) and loblolly pine (*Pinus taeda* L.) in the Southern United States. Early significance in growth faded with time so that after 9 years, vegetation control and genetic enhancement had positive and additive effects on several loblolly pine variables (Pienaar and others 1997). But by far, the major effect was due to vegetation control alone.

Indirect methods—

As noted earlier, mid-May to October often are rainless, and soil moisture is the limiting environmental factor in most of California. Rapid growth of conifer seedlings is best when soil moisture is adequate and sunlight is plentiful, and thus most plantations are located in clearcuttings and recent burns. Competing plant species grow best in this environment as well. Forest vegetation managers have not needed to regenerate areas with intact layers of organic matter or those having a shaded environment. Consequently, they have not developed strategies or methodologies that take advantage of the fact that a layer of organic matter is an inhibitor of seed germination (Click and others 1994, Grime 1979) and that many aggressive shrub species are intolerant of shade (Minore and others 1988) and develop poorly there.

For group-selection cutting, knowledge is needed on the species composition, density, and development of competing vegetation and conifer regeneration. Crucial questions are whether the desired species become established and develop satisfactorily in this environment, and where in it does aggressive competing vegetation develop slowly and conifer seedlings grow well. We have demonstrated that the former happens, but the latter are constrained as well. The key is to find the best opening size/aspect interaction where the environment dampens the growth of competitors more than that of conifer seedlings, particularly those that are tolerant of shade. More work on the topic of natural versus planted seedling growth also would be helpful. On a high-quality site in central California, Heald (1999) found that the height of naturally seeded and planted ponderosa pine seedlings did not differ at the 5-percent level after 9 years. The reason for the dissimilar findings between our study and his is unknown.

Finding this reason will not be an easy task for several reasons: (1) The plant community in group-selection openings typically tends to be large, variable, and of many ages. The more benign environment encourages recruitment of many species and a longer recruitment period than in open plantations. (2) Because of this longer recruitment period and the addition of new and shorter recruits, the standard measures of **average** foliar cover and height are meaningless. A sample of "widest" and "tallest" plants better portrays differences. (3) The more shady environment also may govern what conifer species grows best. For example, after 28 years in the Challenge study, sugar pine (*Pinus lambertiana* Dougl.) and Douglas-fir were 33 percent taller than ponderosa pine (McDonald and Reynolds 1999). (4) Evaluation of the group-selection method probably should not be made in a short timespan. In the small openings at Challenge, the five species of conifers and four species of hardwoods grew at least twice as fast in height the last 18 years as they did the first 10 years. (5) A very large study with sophisticated analytical techniques will be needed. The opening size/distance-from-edge study at Boggs Mountain suggested that many more openings of various sizes on a wide range of aspects and slopes are needed to evaluate these variables and a host of complicated and probably important interactions.

Principles

Nothing is absolute in vegetation management—nature is far too large, complex, and variable to allow "truths" to hold for very long. However, some important principles have evolved from this extensive study that can serve as guides to vegetation managers in the near future:

- The period just after site preparation is probably the most critical because it is here that the growth environment for conifer seedlings can deteriorate most rapidly. Conifer seedling mortality or a slow growth rate is the consequence of inadequate early control of competing vegetation.

- The establishment of individual plants depends on their ability to capture site resources. That means either being present on the site just after disturbance or having the ability to pirate scarce resources from neighbors. This process is most intense soon after site preparation.

- Most species that invade young conifer plantations after disturbance are those that are resistant to disturbance or adapted to it. These species often are characterized by rapid recovery from damage and a high growth rate. The ability to become large quickly, especially belowground, is critical.

The period just after site preparation is probably the most critical because it is here that the growth environment for conifer seedlings can deteriorate most rapidly.

- Biological control of most undesired vegetation often can be achieved if the undesired species arises from seed. However, if it originates from below-ground propagules, like rhizomes, biological control by desirable seeded species, like some forbs and graminoids, is ineffective.

- The population of dormant seeds rarely is exhausted after one disturbance because germination requirements often are polymorphic. This suggests that more than one treatment application may be necessary for control.

Survival of conifer seedlings is seldom a problem if weed control is applied early and is effective, even in drought years.

- Results from many of our studies show that graminoids in young conifer plantations on average to better sites on west-facing slopes of the Cascade and Sierra Nevada Mountains have little effect on the growth of ponderosa pine seedlings, provided that they invade after the pines have become established (McDonald and Fiddler 1986b). However, on the drier east-facing slopes, the graminoids reduce pine growth for scores of years.

Figure 23—This 29-in tall ponderosa pine seedling on a good site has survived in deep shade for 27 years.

- Survival is not a good descriptor of future conifer seedling growth. Ponderosa pine seedlings can live for 27 years or more with 40 needles and 29 in of height (fig. 23).

- Survival of conifer seedlings is seldom a problem if weed control is applied early and is effective, even in drought years.

- Stem diameter of conifer seedlings is a good measure of competition and correlates strongly to it: a small amount of competition equates to rapid diameter growth, and a large amount of competition equates to slow diameter growth.

- Height of young conifer seedlings often is a poor indicator of future growth. Seedlings grow tall for two reasons: (1) because they have plentiful site resources, or (2) because they are forced to grow upward to stay in sunlight (fig. 24). In the latter, the seedlings usually have long, skinny stems that tend to bend or break. Inevitably, height growth of these seedlings slows or ceases until the stem thickens, and the roots and crown develop to the point that they are in balance with the stem.

Figure 24—To stay in sunlight, this Douglas-fir seedling has grown tall and thin.

• Based on 132 regressions involving four shrub variables, three timespans, and three forms of numerical values, foliar cover and crown volume per acre of combined shrubs explained the most variation in most pine parameters (McDonald and Abbott 1997). Because foliar cover is easy to estimate and relate to, it may be the most useful variable from a practical standpoint. Given the choice of average dominant height, density, or foliar cover to evaluate the competitiveness of a plant species, which is best? The height of most forbs and shrubs is governed somewhat like that of the conifer seedlings and hence is a poor descriptor of competitiveness. Density or number of plants per acre is equally poor because it can vary from one to thousands per acre

Because foliar cover is easy to estimate and relate to, it may be the most useful variable from a practical standpoint.

The treated area must be large enough (preferably a 5-ft radius) for the conifer seedling to establish its root system unencumbered for at least the first year and usually for the first 3 years. Early treatment of competing vegetation is extremely important and the most cost effective.

on a single plot, let alone over many plots in several replications. The variation almost always is too high to achieve statistically significant results.

- Because roots of competing plant species rapidly extend into cleared areas and capture valuable site resources, the treated area must be large enough (preferably a 5-ft radius) for the conifer seedling to establish its root system unencumbered for at least the first year and usually for the first 3 years. Early treatment of competing vegetation is extremely important and the most cost effective. Obviously, it is much easier and cheaper to treat competing vegetation when the plants are young and small.

- What constitutes too much competition to conifer seedlings differs with time since planting, number of plants, and species of plants. The first year after planting, one or two perennial woody shrubs with established root systems, but only a few inches tall and within 3 ft of a conifer seedling, are too much. Three sprigs of bearclover and a few small manzanita or ceanothus seedlings within the same distance are too much also. Tappeiner and others (1992) noted that for some shrubs (snowbrush as an example), a stocking rate of two plants per milacre may be sufficient to result in 100 percent cover and maximum leaf area by age 5 or earlier. A general rule of thumb is that competition is too much when the foliar cover of undesirable plants exceeds 10 to 20 percent on poor sites and 20 to 30 percent on good sites.

- Minimizing the amount of competing vegetation often creates an unfavorable habitat for animals and insects that cause problems for regenerating conifers, and allows seedlings to grow rapidly and avoid damage.

- Conifer seedlings stressed for at least 5 years by strong competition are slow to respond to increased resources brought about by removal of the competition. McHenry and Radosevich (1985) noted, "There is abundant evidence from both historical records and research that early competition imposes enormous losses in initial conifer seedling survival and growth." Results also suggest that growth increments continue to be reduced well beyond the first decade of a tree's life. The reason is not fully known, but probably relates to the seedling having to first develop its root system belowground as well as its photosynthetic potential above. Suppressed seedlings have a higher proportion of less photosynthetically efficient foliage than seedlings that are free to grow. Shock to shade-adjusted needles after sudden release also may be a factor. Younger trees do not have this slow-start phenomenon and release quickly and vigorously. This is another reason to release when the conifer seedlings are young.

Growth increments continue to be reduced well beyond the first decade of a tree's life.

- Statistical differences are critical for interpreting study results. Most often, statistical differences in conifer seedling growth occur in 2 to 4 years, particularly if the variable is stem diameter (McDonald and Fiddler 1989) and the test is between the control and the most intensive treatment. Sometimes, a statistical difference at the 5-percent level is delayed and knowing at least three conditions that cause it is important: (1) if the site is of poor quality and the vegetation, including conifer seedlings, grows slowly; (2) if the treatment is only moderately effective and competitive species are present in the treated plots (A corollary to this is that the longer the conifer seedling has to grow with a high level of competition, the longer it takes for a statistically significant difference to occur); (3) if two or three rapidly growing conifer seedlings are growing in the randomly selected control.

- Evaluating the success of a given treatment relates to time since treatment. Visual observations can be misleading, and occasionally even an early statistical difference can disappear in a year or two. In general, treatment evaluation at age 5 is adequate, but at age 10 is better. But even 10 years may not be long enough to evaluate some treatments in some circumstances. In southwestern Oregon, for example, Tesch (1991) noted that Douglas-fir seedlings eventually began to grow well 12 to 15 years after release in a mixed shrub-hardwood community. Another example is from a 10-year study in the southern Cascade Mountains of northern California, where McDonald and Fiddler (1997B) stated that "more time is needed for diameter and height to develop and for relationships to be clarified." Here California red fir seedlings were growing on a poor site in a harsh environment.

- Reforestation success in forest ecosystems with a mediterranean climate depends on the seedlings' ability to successfully compete for soil moisture. This is tempered somewhat by the species' inherent adaptation to withstand moisture stress, and to the increased stress brought about by global warming. Ponderosa and Jeffrey pines, for example, are well adapted to withstand this stress, other conifers less so, with true firs (*Abies* spp.) the least able.

- Short-term seedling-growth goals need to be tempered with longer term considerations that maintain the plant and animal community. During the conifer seedling establishment period, low density and developmental values of competing species are desired, but once the conifer seedlings are growing well, more of some species may be valuable from a practical and ecological viewpoint. Increased density and growth of a given forb or graminoid may be desirable to increase a particular yield from the plantation—sustenance for an endangered species of wildlife, for example.

Challenges

Although much knowledge has been gained, more is needed, and these constitute challenges to future vegetation management endeavors. The challenges are a product of needs originating directly from this study, and suggestions from colleagues in both research and management positions:

- Evaluate individual species or communities of species to determine their degree of competitiveness to young conifer seedlings and to quantify the potential of a species for biological control. The deerbrush versus greenleaf manzanita growth comparison (McDonald and others 1998) is a case in point. On a larger scale, the need is to determine which hardwood, shrub, forb, or graminoid variable (density, foliar cover, height, volume per acre) has the most effect (explains the most variation) in similar pine or fir seedling parameters. Such a determination could indicate which species to control as well as to suggest treatment effectiveness and timing. It could even suggest the "best" species to plant.

- Examine the interaction of various species of conifer seedlings and major competing species (*Arctostaphylos*, *Ceanothus* for example) on a wide range of site qualities.

- The hypothesis that an increasing amount of bare ground, created just after an effective release treatment, increases plant species richness needs to be tested. Conversely, is there an occupied-ground threshold beyond which plant species richness declines? Given the large amount of variation in site quality, species of competing vegetation, and other variables, 10 years is suggested as the time to make this test.

- Better predict what competing plant species, and their potential density and size, will be present in young conifer plantations. We need a better idea of past stand history and number and kind of propagules that are likely to colonize recently disturbed areas.

- Learn more about the belowground ecosystem. Time and again, our statistical analyses and results on conifer seedling/competing plant interactions could explain only so much variation with our aboveground data. More specifically, the number, location, and development patterns of small feeder roots of the most common competing plant species need to be studied. Competition models with the feeder roots of these species and those of conifer seedlings then could be developed. Internal moisture stress of conifer seedlings and competing species would be a valuable adjunct to these studies. Initiation and magnitude of root growth of conifer seedlings relative to that of other vegetation and to soil temperature would also be valuable.

- Mathematical modeling to determine competitive species/growth thresholds is a challenge. The growth simulator "CONIFERS" correlated crown width development of several combined shrubs and hardwoods to several conifer seedling growth variables, and equations suggesting competitive thresholds were determined (Ritchie and Hamann 2006, 2008). More work with additional conifer species and specific competing species would be significant.

- Work on the worth of genetic improvement as a vegetation management tool. Tests with seedlings of different conifer species, more genetically enhanced families, a less aggressive competing species, lower amounts of a competing species, on sites of lower quality need to be done. Conifer seedlings bred specifically for rapid juvenile growth is another potentially worthwhile approach.

- Emphasize autecology and developmental studies that relate conifer seedlings to broad sclerophyll species such as those in the genera *Arctostaphylos*, *Ceanothus*, *Rhamnus*, *Lithocarpus*, *Quercus*, and *Arbutus*, in partially-to-fully shaded plantations. Knowledge on density and growth of graminoids in partial-shade environments relative to that of conifer seedlings is particularly lacking. On a larger scale, begin studies that compare the results of indirect and direct vegetative manipulation in a controlled experiment. Results from indirect vegetation management probably will take longer to achieve than those from direct methods, but the initial (treatment) cost is low. The key is to broaden the research base and evaluate new entities. We would never have known the effects of shade on tanoak, for example, if we had not installed our study.

- Rethink the sometimes negative regard for what are thought of as "weeds." Earlier we noted some species that had biological control and exclusionary value. Other recognized values are for preventing erosion, capture and recycling of nutrients, and improvement of soil chemical and physical properties. However, few species have been evaluated for potential worth by several disciplines. For example, the common weed, rubber rabbitbrush (*Chrysothamnus nauseosus* [Pallas] Britton), provides a good example of potential values: "It includes forage for livestock and wildlife (11.8 percent protein), revegetation of disturbed areas, landscape use, value as potential rubber (7 percent) and resin (up to 35 percent), and application of some of the products for nematocide and antimalarial activity" (Weber and others 1987).

In a similar vein, it is widely recognized that Native Americans valued an amazing number of plant species, sizes, and ages for use in a wide variety of foods, medicines, clothing, shelters, tools, and ceremonies (Anderson 1990). "Going back to the future" could be worthwhile.

- Establish large, long-term studies that evaluate mixes of conifers and competing species in plantations and determine which sequesters the most carbon. What species of vegetation, how much of it, and in what mixture stores the most carbon? For example, do four 20-year rotations of deerbrush and manzanita store more or less carbon than one 80-year rotation of a conifer species? A corollary involves finding a balance between storing carbon and fire hazard. Given the frequency of wildfire in California, storing massive amounts of carbon on the surface of the land for too long, could mean the loss of most of it in a conflagration.

- Encourage related future research, and specifically to provide funding to make this a truly long-term study by safe-guarding and remeasuring many of our study sites at future dates, age 20 for example; and to employ more instruments to gather data such as xylem sap tension of more species, and foliar nutrients of shrubs and graminoids on a range of sites. The values of 20 percent cover on poor sites and 30 percent cover on good sites as being the thresholds beyond which release treatments should be applied also needs to be strengthened with specific studies aimed at doing so.

Conclusions

In many parts of the Western United States, forests of conifer trees stand at the pinnacle of plant succession. These trees and the forest ecosystems that they form constitute places where plants and animals flourish, the soil provides valuable nutrients and moisture, and water flows from the land in a gentle and measured way. Unfortunately, wildfires and harvesting without adequate reforestation have left large tracts of forest land in California with few or no trees, and large areas inhabited by brush and weeds. In these areas, plant and animal diversity is much reduced and fewer plant communities and habitats are present. Plainly, these lands are not producing the variety of benefits, goods, and services that today's public demands. This paper brings together the results of our study on plantation release in an effort to alleviate this problem and to start these lands toward attaining full productivity. In places, it also "passes the torch" to scientists and managers by bringing attention to new and different approaches to vegetation management.

> **Given the frequency of wildfire in California, storing massive amounts of carbon on the surface of the land for too long, could mean the loss of most of it in a conflagration.**

This paper and the publications upon which it is based, have both scientists and managers as their audience. Some are aimed at one or the other, but in general, a scientific finding quickly becomes useful to the manager, and no attempt has been made to specify either audience. Similarly, this paper should interest vegetation managers, botanists, and ecologists as the primary audience, followed closely by range and wildlife managers. Fuel and fire researchers and managers also should find the developmental tables on various species of vegetation useful because volumes per acre over various timespans can be calculated. Also as the various species of vegetation develop, the amount of carbon that is sequestered can be ascertained as well. Because of the large variety of disciplines in the audience, no attempt has been made to prioritize the principles or the challenges. The intent is that they or pieces of them will be useful to all.

Results from more than 25 years of research, 30 study areas, and 60 publications have answered many questions on the development of plant communities in young conifer plantations, when and where they develop, and how they influence young conifer seedlings. But judging from the challenges above, much more needs to be done. Indeed, for every question answered, several more arise. The need for vegetation management research never ends. This is the first of several overarching conclusions.

Aldo Leopold once said "The first rule of intelligent tinkering in nature is to keep all the pieces." Our goal in this study was to bring a more holistic perspective to the art of managing vegetation. Consequently, we present detailed material on the plant communities that are present in young conifer plantations and the biological influences that shape them. We believe that this material is necessary to understand the effectiveness of the operational techniques that we used. In this sense, we kept all the pieces.

Of the direct release techniques that we tested, herbicides were the most effective biologically, largely because they "worked" both above- and belowground. They tended to kill undesirable plants and consequently provided additional moisture and nutrients to conifer seedlings. A general ranking of our treatments from biologically effective to ineffective following herbicides are large mulches and large-area manual grubbing, mechanical, grazing, small mulches, small grubbed areas, and control (McDonald and Fiddler 1993b). A general trend for cost is low for herbicides and grazing, increases with size of area treated by grubbing and mulches, decreases with size of area treated with large machines, and is highest for grubbing large areas or applying large mulches.

A general ranking of our treatments from biologically effective to ineffective following herbicides are large mulches and large-area manual grubbing, mechanical, grazing, small mulches, small grubbed areas, and control.

All of the release treatments that vegetation managers have at their command have degrees of application and at least one limitation. No treatment is immune to causing too much disturbance to the environment, or being too costly, or not being socially acceptable, or simply being limited by the steepness of slope or rocky ground. All are subject to some degree of risk, regulation, or creating conditions that will be difficult to manage in the future. In almost all instances, however, the ecological implications of manipulating the vegetation are more favorable than doing nothing (fig. 25).

Figure 25—This fully stocked and rapidly growing plantation in a clearcutting will soon be a forest with many more options for managing the ecosystem than if it had not been treated.

Successful ecosystem management includes the ability to predict the plant species, density, and developmental trends of future plant communities.

Good vegetation management fits well into good ecosystem management, and many inferences for enhancing ecosystem management have been presented in this paper. Two stand out: plant species succession and carbon sequestration. Successful ecosystem management includes the ability to predict the plant species, density, and developmental trends of future plant communities. As Taylor and others (2008) noted "Projecting forest succession has become an increasingly relevant component of ecosystem management." For sequestering carbon, new forests begin to accumulate carbon rapidly, both aboveground in crowns and boles, and belowground in new root systems. Thus it is important to establish vigorous stands, keep them healthy, and growing well. Of course, establishing new, fully stocked, rapidly growing stands is a major goal of vegetation management. Indeed, "reduced deforestation, fast-growing plantations, and agroforestry could contribute 12 to 15 percent towards offsetting global carbon emissions. It is good business ecologically and may catch the conscience of the public" (Powers 2004).

Another yield from forest land is becoming critical, and that is water. As noted in the Redding Record Searchlight (2009), "With our [changing] weather patterns, with climate change, and our population growth, we've got to look at how we use every drop," and "Facing a third dry year and record-low reservoirs, the Bureau of Reclamation announced major water cuts last month in California." Grant (2008) stated "In the not so distant future, clean water will be the single most important commodity produced from national forest lands. It will totally eclipse timber." Some basic research in the form of questions needs to be done: (1) Which herbaceous, hardwood, and conifer species uses less water? (2) Can a conifer plantation be planted and managed for both timber production and water yield? (3) Can the ensuing forest be cut in such a way as to provide more high-quality water later in the spring when it is most needed? (4) How can the conifer seedlings and inevitable competing vegetation from this cutting be manipulated to maintain increased growth and water yield?

Results from the direct release methods that we tested remain viable today. For example, the herbicides that we studied are still being used. New ones have been formulated, but they tend to be variations of those we used, perhaps with application to a broader range of competing species or to one or two target species. Planting through slash and eliminating at least some site preparation is being increasingly used today. It leaves much organic material on the ground that inhibits the germination of seeds of competing species. In terms of regeneration, this form of indirect vegetation management is a gain: in terms of fire hazard it is an added risk.

In their book on forest vegetation management for conifer production, Walstad and Kuch (1987) stated that quantitative models, which forecast the long-term effect of competing vegetation on stand development, are generally lacking. To correct this deficiency, they recommended that treatments should be evaluated for their (1) ability to suppress competing vegetation, (2) effect on economic crop, (3) cost effectiveness, and (4) protection of site resources and other values. This paper contributes at least some knowledge to each of these recommendations.

Given 50 or more years of vegetation management in California, have the plant species that vigorously compete with young conifer seedlings been markedly affected by all the work that has been done? More specifically, have all the release techniques that have been used given vegetation managers an "edge" over the many adaptations and capabilities of these species and the communities in which they reside? Based on our extensive observations and sampling throughout northern and central California, the best answer is "probably," but only temporarily. Not all areas in a plantation are treated, and islands of competing vegetation remain. In addition, buried seeds in the soil and rhizomes from edge vegetation can lead to invasion in a matter of months. In the short term, and with vigilance, vegetation mangers have an edge, but in the long term, the presence and capability of competing species remains unaltered across the landscape.

Occasionally, opponents of intensive forest management want to remove or severely limit some of the techniques that vegetation managers use. This seems paradoxical. Today, the vegetation manager is bombarded from every direction. Forest managers, biologists, environmentalists, economists, and politicians demand special consideration. We have shown in this paper that almost all of the treatment alternatives that we examined have application, or at least feasibility, in some sense. In this ever-more-complex world with its myriad of demands, the manager needs more tools and methods, not fewer. A major conclusion drawn from our research is that plantations in clearcuttings, herbicides, burning, and grazing are feasible at some place, at some time, and for some purpose. They should remain in the vegetation manager's repertory of available methods and techniques.

Acknowledgments

The authors thank Richard Fitzgerald, John Fiske, and Bill Merrihew for their thoughtful, insightful, and comprehensive reviews. We also are grateful to Todd Hamilton for producing the computer-assisted charts and figures.

Metric Equivalents

When you know:	Multiply by:	To find:
Inches (in)	2.54	Centimeters
Feet (ft)	.305	Meters
Miles (mi)	1.609	Kilometers
Acre	.405	Hectares
Square feet (ft^2)	.0929	Square meters
Square feet per acre (ft^2 per acre)	.229	Square meters per hectare
Cubic feet (ft^3)	.0283	Cubic meters
Degrees Fahrenheit (°F)	.55(°F − 32)	Degrees Celsius

Literature Cited

Anderson, M.K. 1990. California Indian horticulture. Fremontia. 18(20): 7–14.

Antos, J.A.; Halpern, C.B. 1997. Root system differences among species: implications for early successional changes in forests of western Oregon. American Midland Naturalist. 138: 97–108.

Atzet, T.; Martin, R.E. 1992. Natural disturbance regimes in the Klamath Province. In: Kerner, H.M., ed. Proceedings of the symposium on biodiversity of northwestern California. Rep. 29. Berkeley, CA: Wildland Resources Center, University of California: 40–48.

Bedard, W.D.; Robertson, A.S.; Ferrell, G.T. 1989. Growth loss in sapling ponderosa pine associated with injury caused by the gouty pitch midge. In: Alfaro, R.I.; Glover, S.G., eds. Proceedings of a meeting of the International Union of Forestry Research Organization working group on insects affecting reforestation; Victoria, BC: Forestry Canada, Pacific Forestry Centre: 196–204.

Bruce, H.D. 1936. Summary of stump eradication experiments. Typewritten report on file with Philip McDonald, Pacific Southwest Research Station, 3644 Avtech Parkway, Redding, CA 96002. 37 p.

Campbell, R.A. 1991. Silvicultural herbicides in Canada: registration status and research trends. The Forestry Chronicle. 67(5): 520–527.

Click, C.; Fiske, J.; Macmeeken, S.; Sherlock, J. 1994. Alternatives to herbicides in the USDA Forest Service Pacific Southwest Region—the ten-year update. In: Proceedings of the 15th annual forest vegetation management conference. Redding, CA: Forest Vegetation Management Conference: 46–60.

Click, C.; Fiske, J.N.; Sherlock, J.; Wescom, R. 1989. Alternatives to herbicides—update based on the five-year herbicide use moratorium in the USDA Forest Service Pacific Southwest Region. In: Proceedings of the 10th annual forest vegetation management conference. Redding, CA: Forest Vegetation Management Conference: 49–90.

Connell, J.H.; Slatyer, R.O. 1977. Mechanisms of succession in natural communities and their role in community stability and organization. American Naturalist. 111: 1119–1144.

Crouch, G.L. 1979. Atrazine improves survival and growth of ponderosa pine threatened by vegetative competition and pocket gophers. Forest Science. 25(1): 99–111.

Daubenmire, R.F. 1968. Plant communities: a textbook on plant synecology. New York: Harper and Row. 300 p.

Eissenstat, D.M.; Mitchell, J.E. 1983. Effects of seeding grass and clover on growth and water potential of Douglas-fir seedlings. Forest Science. 29(1): 166–179.

Fiddler, G.O.; McDonald, P.M. 1987. Alternative treatments for releasing conifer seedlings: a study update. In: Proceedings of the 8th annual forest vegetation management conference. Redding, CA: Forest Vegetation Management Conference: 64–69.

Fiddler, G.O.; McDonald, P.M. 1990. Manual release contracting: production rates, costs, and future. Western Journal of Applied Forestry. 5(3): 83–85.

Fiddler, G.O.; McDonald, P.M. 1997. Mechanical and chemical release in a 12-year-old ponderosa pine plantation. Res. Pap. PSW-RP-232. Albany, CA: U.S. Department of Agriculture, Forest Service, Pacific Southwest Research Station. 12 p.

Fiddler, G.O.; McDonald, P.M.; Mori, S.R. 2000. Mechanical and chemical release applied to a 16-year-old pine plantation. Res. Note PSW-RN-425. Albany, CA: U.S. Department of Agriculture, Forest Service, Pacific Southwest Research Station. 11 p.

Furniss, R.L.; Carolin, V.M. 1977. Western forest insects. Misc. Publ. 1339. Washington, DC: U.S. Department of Agriculture, Forest Service. p. 68.

Grant, G. 2008. National forest lands and water supplies in an uncertain climate future. In: Mazza, R., ed. Science Update. Issue 16. Portland, OR: U.S. Department of Agriculture, Forest Service, Pacific Northwest Research Station. p. 6.

Grime, J.P. 1979. Plant strategies and vegetation processes. New York: John Wiley and Sons. 222 p.

Grinnell, J. 1936. Up-hill planters. The Condor. 38: 80–82.

Heald, R.C. 1999. Personal communication. Blodgett Forest Research Station, Center for Forestry, University of California. 4501 Blodgett Forest Road, Georgetown, CA 95634.

Hickman, J.C., ed. 1993. The Jepson manual, higher plants of California. Berkeley: University of California Press. 1400 p.

Krueger, W.C. 1983. Cattle grazing in managed forests. In: Roche, B.F., Jr.; Baumgartner, D.M., comps. and eds. Proceedings of the symposium on forestland grazing. Pullman, WA: Washington State University: 29–42.

Little, E.L., Jr. 1979. Checklist of the United States trees (native and naturalized). Agric. Handb. 541. Washington, DC: U.S. Department of Agriculture, Forest Service. 375 p.

Logan, R. 1982. Grass adaptations and their impact on conifer seedlings. Delivered at a workshop on weed ecology, Grants Pass, OR, November 9, 1982. On file with: Philip McDonald, Pacific Southwest Research Station, 3644 Avtech Parkway, Redding, CA 96002.

McDonald, P.M. 1978. Silviculture-ecology of three native California hardwoods on high sites in north-central California. Corvallis, OR: Oregon State University. 309 p. Ph.D. dissertation.

McDonald, P.M. 1982. Grasses in young conifer plantations—hindrance and help. Northwest Science. 60(4): 271–278.

McDonald, P.M. 1983. Clearcutting and natural regeneration: management implications for the northern Sierra Nevada. Gen. Tech. Rep. PSW-70. Berkeley, CA: U.S. Department of Agriculture, Forest Service, Pacific Southwest Research Station. 11 p.

McDonald, P.M. 1999. Diversity, density, and development of early vegetation in a small clear-cut environment. Res. Pap. PSW-RP-239. Albany, CA: U.S. Department of Agriculture, Forest Service, Pacific Southwest Research Station. 22 p.

McDonald, P.M. 2003. Development of a mixed-shrub–planted ponderosa pine community on a poor site after site preparation and release. Res. Pap. PSW-RP-248. Albany, CA: U.S. Department of Agriculture, Forest Service, Pacific Southwest Research Station. 28 p.

McDonald, P.M.; Abbott, C.S. 1994. Seedfall, regeneration, and seedling development in group-selection openings. Res. Pap. PSW-RP-220. Albany, CA: U.S. Department of Agriculture, Forest Service, Pacific Southwest Research Station. 13 p.

McDonald, P.M.; Abbott, C.S. 1997. Vegetation trends in a 31-year-old ponderosa pine plantation: effect of different shrub densities. Res. Pap. PSW-RP-231. Albany, CA: U.S. Department of Agriculture, Forest Service, Pacific Southwest Research Station. 35 p.

McDonald, P.M.; Abbott, C.S.; Fiddler, G.O. 1999a. Development of a shrub-fern-ponderosa pine community eleven years after site preparation and release. Western Journal of Applied Forestry. 14(4): 194–199.

McDonald, P.M.; Anderson, P.J.; Fiddler, G.O. 1997. Vegetation in group-selection openings: early trends. Res. Note PSW-RN-421. Albany, CA: U.S. Department of Agriculture, Forest Service, Pacific Southwest Research Station. 7 p.

McDonald, P.M.; Everest, G.A. 1996. Response of young ponderosa pines, shrubs, and grasses to two release treatments. Res. Note PSW-RN-419. Albany, CA: U.S. Department of Agriculture, Forest Service, Pacific Southwest Research Station. 7 p.

McDonald, P.M.; Fiddler, G.O. 1986a. Release of Douglas-fir seedlings: growth and treatment costs. Res. Pap. PSW-182. Berkeley, CA: U.S. Department of Agriculture, Forest Service, Pacific Southwest Research Station. 9 p.

McDonald, P.M.; Fiddler, G.O. 1986b. Weed treatment strategies to control losses in ponderosa pine plantations. In: Helgerson, O.T., ed. Proceedings of a workshop on forest pest management in southwest Oregon. Corvallis, OR: Oregon State University: 47–53.

McDonald, P.M.; Fiddler, G.O. 1989. Competing vegetation in ponderosa pine plantations: ecology and control. Gen. Tech. Rep. PSW-113. Berkeley, CA: U.S. Department of Agriculture, Forest Service, Pacific Southwest Research Station. 26 p.

McDonald, P.M.; Fiddler, G.O. 1990. Ponderosa pine seedlings and competing vegetation: ecology, growth, and cost. Res. Pap. PSW-199. Berkeley, CA: U.S. Department of Agriculture, Forest Service, Pacific Southwest Research Station. 10 p.

McDonald, P.M.; Fiddler, G.O. 1993a. Vegetative trends in a young conifer plantation after 10 years of grazing by sheep. Res. Pap. PSW-RP-215. Albany, CA: U.S. Department of Agriculture, Forest Service, Pacific Southwest Research Station. 9 p.

McDonald, P.M.; Fiddler, G.O. 1993b. Feasibility of alternatives to herbicides in young conifer plantations in California. Canadian Journal of Forest Research. 23: 2015–2022.

McDonald, P.M.; Fiddler, G.O. 1995. Development of a mixed shrub–ponderosa pine community in a natural and treated condition. Res. Pap. PSW-224. Albany, CA: U.S. Department of Agriculture, Forest Service, Pacific Southwest Research Station. 19 p.

McDonald, P.M.; Fiddler, G.O. 1996. Development of a mixed shrub–tanoak–Douglas-fir community in a treated and untreated condition. Res. Pap. PSW-RP-225. Albany, CA: U.S. Department of Agriculture, Forest Service, Pacific Southwest Research Station. 16 p.

McDonald, P.M.; Fiddler, G.O. 1997b. Treatment duration and time since disturbance affect vegetation development in a young California red fir plantation. Res. Pap. PSW-RP-233. Albany, CA: U.S. Department of Agriculture, Forest Service, Pacific Southwest Research Station. 14 p.

McDonald, P.M.; Fiddler, G.O. 1997. Vegetation trends in a young ponderosa pine plantation treated by manual release and mulching. Res. Pap. PSW-RP-234. Albany, CA: U.S. Department of Agriculture, Forest Service, Pacific Southwest Research Station. 15 p.

McDonald, P.M.; Fiddler, G.O. 1999a. Effect of cattle grazing, seeded grass, and an herbicide on ponderosa pine seedling survival and growth. Res. Pap. PSW-RP-242. Albany, CA: U.S. Department of Agriculture, Forest Service, Pacific Southwest Research Station. 15 p.

McDonald, P.M.; Fiddler, G.O. 1999b. Ecology and development of Douglas-fir seedlings and associated plant species in a Coast Range plantation. Res. Pap. PSW-RP-243. Albany, CA: U.S. Department of Agriculture, Forest Service, Pacific Southwest Research Station. 18 p.

McDonald, P.M.; Fiddler, G.O. 1999c. Recovery of a bearclover (*Chamaebatia foliolosa*) plant community after site preparation and planting of ponderosa pine seedlings. Res. Note PSW-RN-423. Albany, CA: U.S. Department of Agriculture, Forest Service, Pacific Southwest Research Station. 7 p.

McDonald, P.M.; Fiddler, G.O. 2001a. Timing and duration of release affect vegetation development in a young California white fir plantation. Res. Pap. PSW-RP-246. Albany, CA: U.S. Department of Agriculture, Forest Service, Pacific Southwest Research Station. 15 p.

McDonald, P.M.; Fiddler, G.O. 2001a. Timing and duration of release affect vegetation development in a young ponderosa pine plantation. Res. Pap. PSW-RP-245. Albany, CA: U.S. Department of Agriculture, Forest Service, Pacific Southwest Research Station. 14 p.

McDonald, P.M.; Fiddler, G.O. 2001b. Changes in plant communities after planting and release of conifer seedlings: early findings. In: Barras, S.J. ed., Proceedings of the national silvicultural workshop. RMRS-P-19. Fort Collins, CO: U.S. Department of Agriculture, Forest Service, Rocky Mountain Research Station: 26–31.

McDonald, P.M.; Fiddler, G.O. 2002. Relationship of native and introduced grasses with and without cattle in a young ponderosa pine plantation. Western Journal of Applied Forestry. 17(1): 31–36.

McDonald, P.M.; Fiddler, G.O. 2006. Plant species diversity in young conifer plantations in northern and central California. Western Journal of Applied Forestry. 21(1): 49–54.

McDonald, P.M.; Fiddler, G.O. 2007. Development of vegetation in a young ponderosa pine plantation: effect of treatment duration and time since disturbance. Res. Pap. PSW-RP-251. Albany, CA: U.S. Department of Agriculture, Forest Service, Pacific Southwest Research Station. 23 p.

McDonald, P.M.; Fiddler, G.O.; Harrison, H.H. 1994a. Mulching to regenerate a harsh site: effect on Douglas-fir seedlings, forbs, grasses, and ferns. Res. Pap. PSW-RP-222. Albany, CA: U.S. Department of Agriculture, Forest Service, Pacific Southwest Research Station. 10 p.

McDonald, P.M.; Fiddler, G.O.; Henry, W.T. 1994b. Large mulches and manual release enhance growth of ponderosa pine seedlings. New Forests. 8: 169–178.

McDonald, P.M.; Fiddler, G.O.; Kitzmiller, J.H. 1994c. Genetically improved ponderosa pine seedlings outgrow nursery-run seedlings with and without competition—early findings. Western Journal of Applied Forestry. 9(2): 57–61.

McDonald, P.M.; Fiddler, G.O.; Meyer, P.W. 1996. Vegetation trends in a young conifer plantation after grazing, grubbing, and chemical release. Res. Pap. PSW-RP-228. Albany, CA: U.S. Department of Agriculture, Forest Service, Pacific Southwest Research Station. 17 p.

McDonald, P.M.; Fiddler, G.O.; Potter, D.A. 2004. Ecology and manipulation of bearclover (*Chamaebatia foliolosa*) in northern and central California: the status of our knowledge. Gen. Tech. Rep. PSW-GTR-190. Albany, CA: U.S. Department of Agriculture, Forest Service, Pacific Southwest Research Station. 26 p.

McDonald, P.M.; Fiddler, G.O.; Ritchie, M.W.; Anderson, P.J. 2009. Naturally seeded versus planted ponderosa pine seedlings in group-selection openings. Western Journal of Applied Forestry. 24(1): 48–54.

McDonald, P.M.; Fiddler, G.O.; Smith, W.H. 1989. Mulches and manual release fail to enhance Douglas-fir seedling survival and growth. In: Proceedings of the 10th annual forest vegetation management conference. Redding, CA: Forest Vegetation Management Conference: 140–153.

McDonald, P.M.; Fiske, J.N. 2000. An indirect strategy for controlling undesirable vegetation in young conifer stands. In: Proceedings of the 3rd annual PNW-Integrated Vegetation Management Association forestry and rights-of-way conference. Pullman, WA: Washington State University: 46–51.

McDonald, P.M.; Helgerson, O.T. 1990. Mulches aid in regenerating California and Oregon forests: past, present, and future. Gen. Tech. Rep. PSW-123. Berkeley, CA: U.S. Department of Agriculture, Forest Service, Pacific Southwest Research Station. 19 p.

McDonald, P.M.; Laurie, W.D.; Hill, R. 1998. Early growth characteristics of planted deerbrush and greenleaf manzanita seedlings in California. Res. Note PSW-RN-422. Albany, CA: U.S. Department of Agriculture, Forest Service, Pacific Southwest Research Station. 6 p.

McDonald, P.M.; Mori, S.R.; Fiddler, G.O. 1999b. Effect of competition on genetically improved ponderosa pine seedlings. Canadian Journal of Forest Research. 29: 940–946.

McDonald, P.M.; Radosevich, S.R. 1992. General principles of vegetation management. Chapter 4. In: Silvicultural approaches to animal damage management in Pacific Northwest forests. Gen. Tech. Rep. PNW-GTR-287. Portland, OR: U.S. Department of Agriculture, Forest Service, Pacific Northwest Research Station: 67–91.

McDonald, P.M.; Reynolds, P.E. 1999. Plant community development after 28 years in small group-selection openings. Res. Pap. PSW-RP-241. Albany, CA: U.S. Department of Agriculture, Forest Service, Pacific Southwest Research Station. 17 p.

McDonald, P.M.; Tappeiner, J.C., II. 1986. Weeds: life cycles suggest controls. Journal of Forestry. 84(10): 33–37.

McDonald, P.M.; Tappeiner, J.C., II. 2002. California's hardwood resource: seeds, seedlings, and sprouts of three important forest-zone species. Gen Tech. Rep. PSW-GTR-185. Albany, CA: U.S. Department of Agriculture, Forest Service, Pacific Southwest Research Station. 39 p.

McHenry, W.B.; Radosevich, S.R. 1985. Forest vegetation management. In: California weed conference, sponsors. Principles of weed control in California. Fresno, CA: Thompson Publications: 400–413.

Minore, D.; Weatherly, H.G.; Means, J.E. 1988. Growth of whiteleaf manzanita (*Arctostaphylos viscida* Parry). Forest Science. 34(4): 1094–1100.

Mooney, H.A.; Dunn, E.L. 1970. Convergent evolution of Mediterranean-climate evergreen schlerophyll shrubs. Evolution. 24: 293–303.

Morris, W.F.; Wood, D.M. 1989. The role of lupine in succession on Mount St. Helens: facilitation or inhibition? Ecology. 70(3): 697–703.

Odum, E.P. 1969. The strategy of ecosystem development. Science. 164: 262–270.

Perry, D.A. 1994. Forest ecosystems. Baltimore, MD: John Hopkins University Press. 165 p.

Pienaar, L.V.; Shiver, B.D.; Harrison, W.M. 1997. Loblolly pine improved planting stock—vegetation control study, age 9 results. PMRC Tech. Pap. No. 1997-2. Athens, GA: Daniel B. Warnell School of Forest Resources, University of Georgia. 17 p.

Powers, R.F. 2004. World trends in forests, forest use, wood supply; the irony of California forestry; the challenge to our profession. In: Proceedings of the 24th annual forest vegetation management conference. Redding, CA: Forest Vegetation Management Conference: 1–17.

Powers, R.F.; Ferrell, G.T. 1996. Moisture, nutrient, and insect constraints on plantation growth: The "Garden of Eden" study. New Zealand Journal of Forestry Science. 26(1/2): 126–144.

Powers, R.F.; Oliver, W.W. 1978. Site classification of ponderosa pine stands under stocking control in California. Res. Pap. PSW-128. Berkeley, CA: U.S. Department of Agriculture, Forest Service, Pacific Southwest Research Station. 9 p.

Radosevich, S.R. 1984. Interference between greenleaf manzanita (*Arctostaphylos patula*) and ponderosa pine (*Pinus ponderosa*). In: Duryea, M.; Brown, G. eds. Seedling physiology and reforestation success. Dordrecht, The Netherlands: Martinus Nijoff/Junk: 259–270.

Radosevich, S.R.; Holt, J.S. 1984. Weed ecology, implications for vegetation management. New York: John Wiley and Sons. 57 p.

Redding [CA] Record Searchlight. 2009. Farm subsidies turn on water use debate. April 15; Sect. A1, A6.

Reice, S.R. 1994. Nonequilibrium determinants of biological community structure. American Scientist. 82: 424–435.

Ritchie, M.W.; Hamann, J.D. 2006. Modeling dynamics of competing vegetation in young conifer plantations of northern California and southern Oregon, USA. Canadian Journal of Forest Research. 36: 2523–2532.

Ritchie, M.W.; Hamann, J.D. 2008. Individual tree height-diameter-crown width increment equations for young Douglas-fir plantations. New Forests. 35: 173–186.

Rosenthal, S.S.; Maddox, D.M.; Brunetti, K. 1985. Biological control methods. In: Principles of weed control in California. Fresno, CA: California Weed Conference: 66–94.

Roy, D.F. 1955. Hardwood sprout measurements in northwestern California. Res. Note 95. Berkeley, CA: U.S. Department of Agriculture, Forest Service, California Forest and Range Experiment Station. 6 p.

Scholander, P.F.; Hammel, H.T.; Bradstreet, E.D.; Hemingsen, E.A. 1965. Sap pressure in vascular plants. Science. 148: 339–346.

Sharrow, S.H. 1994. Sheep as a silvicultural management tool in temperate conifer forests. Sheep Research Journal. (special issue).

Skinner, C.N.; Taylor, A.H. 2006. Southern Cascades bioregion. In: Sugihara, N.G.; van Wagtendonk, J.; Fites-Kaufman, J.; Shaffer, K.; Thode, A.E., eds. Fire in California's ecosystems. Berkeley, CA: University of California Press: 195–224.

Stebbins, G.L. 1972. Evolution and diversity of arid-land shrubs. In: McKell, C.M.; Blaisdell, J.P.; Goodin, J.R., tech. eds. Gen. Tech. Rep. INT-1. Ogden, UT: U.S. Department of Agriculture, Forest Service, Intermountain Forest and Range Experiment Station: 111–120.

Stevens, R.E. 1959. Biology and control of the pine needle-sheath miner (*Zelleria haimbachi* Busch). Tech. Pap. 30. Berkeley, CA: U.S. Department of Agriculture, Forest Service, Pacific Southwest Research Station. 20 p.

Stewart, R.E.; Gross, L.L.; Honkala, B.H. 1984. Effects of competing vegetation on forest trees: a bibliography with abstracts. Gen. Tech. Rep. WO-43. Washington, DC: U.S. Department of Agriculture, Forest Service.

Tappeiner, J.C., II; McDonald, P.M. 1984. Development of tanoak understories in conifer stands. Canadian Journal of Forest Research. 14: 271–277.

Tappeiner, J.C., II; McDonald, P.M.; Roy, D.F. 1990. *Lithocarpus densiflorous* (Hook. & Arn.) Rehd., tanoak. In: Burns, R.M.; Honkala, B.H., tech. coords. Silvics of North America. Volume 2. Hardwoods. Agric. Handb. 654. Washington, DC: U.S. Department of Agriculture, Forest Service: 417–425.

Tappeiner, J.C., II; Newton, M.; McDonald, P.M.; Harrington, T.B. 1992. Ecology of hardwoods, shrubs, and herbaceous vegetation: effect on conifer regeneration. In: Hobbs, S.D.; Tesch, S.D.; Owston, P.W.; Stewart, R.E.; Tappeiner, J.C., II; Wells, G.E., eds. Reforestation practices in southwestern Oregon and northern California. Corvallis, OR: Forest Research Laboratory, Oregon State University: 136–164. Chapter 7.

Taylor, A.R.; Chen, H.Y.H.; VanDamme, L. 2008. A review of forest succession models and their suitability for forest management planning. Forest Science. 55(1): 23–36.

Tesch, S.D. 1991. Personal communication. Forestry intensified research program, College of Forestry, Oregon State University, 3200 SW Jefferson Way, Corvallis, OR 97331.

Tesch, S.D.; Hobbs, S.D. 1989. Impact of shrub sprout competition on Douglas-fir seedling development. Western Journal of Applied Forestry. 4(3): 89–92.

Trappe, J.M. 1981. Mycorrhizae and productivity of arid and semiarid rangelands. In: Manassah, J.T.; Briskey, E.J. eds. Advances in food producing systems for arid and semiarid lands. New York: Academic Press, Inc.: 581–599.

Walstad, J.D.; Kuch, P.J. 1987. Forest vegetation management for conifer production. New York: John Wiley and Sons. 523 p.

Waring, R.H.; Cleary, B.D. 1967. Plant moisture stress: evaluation by pressure bomb. Science. 155: 1248–1254.

Weber, D.J.; Hegerhorst, D.F.; Davis, T.D.; McArthur, E.D. 1987. Potential uses of rubber rabbitbrush (*Chrysothamnus nauseosus*). In: Johnson, K.L., ed. In: Proceedings of the fourth Utah shrub ecology workshop. Logan, UT: Utah State University: 27–33.

Wilkinson, W.H.; McDonald, P.M.; Morgan, P. 1997. Tanoak sprout development after cutting and burning in a shade environment. Western Journal of Applied Forestry. 12(1): 21–26.